Sound Synthesis

Analog and Digital Techniques

Sound Synthesis

Analog and Digital Techniques

Terence Thomas

TAB BOOKS Inc.
Blue Ridge Summit, PA

FIRST EDITION / FIRST PRINTING

© 1990 by **TAB BOOKS Inc.**
Printed in the United States of America

Library of Congress Cataloging-in-Publication Data

Thomas, Terence, 1942 –
    Synthesis : analog and digital techniques / by Terence Thomas.
      p.   cm.
    ISBN 0-8306-9276-2 :   ISBN 0-8306-3276-X (pbk.)
    1. Digital circuits—Design and construction.   2. Synthesizer
(Musical instrument)   3. MIDI (Standard)   I. Title.
TK7868.D5T49 1990
786.7′4—dc20   89-20464
                                                      CIP

TAB BOOKS Inc. offers software for sale. For information and a catalog, please contact TAB Software Department, Blue Ridge Summit, PA 17294-0850.

Questions regarding the content of this book should be addressed to:

Reader Inquiry Branch
TAB BOOKS Inc.
Blue Ridge Summit, PA 17294-0850

Acquisitions Editor: Roland S. Phelps
Book Editor and Designer: Lisa A. Doyle
Production: Katherine Brown

Contents

Introduction

Synthesizers have had and will continue to have a most profound effect on the music world. Modern technology has revolutionized the recording industry and has changed the way we make music. These advances, spurred on by the industries' active research and development programs, are nothing short of phenomenal. A veritable avalanche of digital synthesizers and sound-processing equipment has inundated the music market and presented the prospective buyer with a plethora of systems and techniques.

It is the purpose of this book to clear up some of the confusion and provide the reader with an anatomy of analog and digital synthesizer systems. Starting with power requirements, Chapter 1 is on synthesizer power supplies. The next chapter is on waveshape generation, with both audio frequency as well as low-frequency control voltage sources. Although many oscillator designs (both analog and digital) have been proposed, none are superior to the sawtooth design in Chapter 2.

Chapter 3 is on filters and other versatile tone modification circuits. Chapter 4 discusses the subject of exponential control-voltage generation extensively because it is the single most important element in sound synthesis, and high-speed control-voltage generation provides the key to the most advanced and sophisticated level of tonal experimentation. Add to this a multistage voltage-variable envelope generator (Chapter 5) and you leave little to be desired when it comes to the production of electronic sound.

Keyboards and other manual control devices are then covered in Chapter 7 including a home-brew ribbon controller, which is made of common household materials. Any conceivable control-voltage parameter can be attained by the use of devices in Chapter 8, Attenuators and Processors. (The chapter on amplifiers also covers preamplifiers, voltage-controlled amplifiers, and even a device that is designed to recover and reproduce concert-hall ambience that is normally lost in the recording process.) Feedback principles such as dual-loop interlock and link coordination are discussed as well as many other advanced control techniques.

Some unique designs are included in Chapter 9, Miscellaneous Circuits, such as a voltage-controlled reverb, an octavizer, and a simple flanger. Other circuits of interest in that chapter are a control-voltage inverter, a programmable panning circuit, and an envelope detector. Voltage-control techniques are applied to as many circuit elements as possible to accommodate new methods of synchronization and to maximize module efficiency.

No book about synthesizers would be complete without a discussion of the Musical Instrument Digital Interface (MIDI) system (Chapter 11), which includes one important addition—a digital-to-analog MIDI interface. The MIDI system was devised as a communication system for digital equipment, but the MIDI interface presented provides analog equipment with the opportunity to participate in this electronic conversation. The interface can also be used to expand the tonal and envelope control potential of any digital synthesizer.

If you intend to take advantage of the designs in this book, a certain amount of circuit construction will be necessary. Chapter 1 contains information on what you will need for projects as well as some helpful suggestions to get you started. The component mapping and parts identification chapter (13) can also be of special interest to anyone contemplating project construction. If this is your first experience with circuit building, it might be a good idea to pick up a book on basic circuits and wiring techniques. For the more experienced and ambitious, the chapter on systems planning (Chapter 10) contains design details for two complete synthesizer systems, including the cabinets and front panel layouts. The foil patterns provided throughout the book help to assure efficient component layout and proper circuit operation and can be used as a guide for your own designs. Or, you can choose pre-etched circuit boards, available at local electronic suppliers.

For those who show no propensity to build their own equipment, Chapter 12 explains modulation techniques used in digital synthesizers. The "patch" diagrams can open up new possibilities for digital and analog interfacing and at the same time stimulate the imagination. Understanding circuit designs, whether or not you intend to build them, can expand your concepts and enable you to achieve your most ambitious goals.

Another major development from digital research is the sampler (sampling synthesizer), and they come in a wide variety of sizes and prices. The larger and more expensive machines can produce superior quality and a greater number of effects, but with the use of external modules and unusual patching arrangements for both input and output element modification, you can produce, with even the most inexpensive sampler, results that are amazingly comparable to more elaborate sampling synthesizers.

Those considering purchasing a unit should find that the information in the following pages can better prepare them to make intelligent decisions when selecting a commercial synthesizer. Choosing the best equipment for your needs and budget can be an overwhelming experience because of the enormous inventory of equipment available.

The circuits described herein are of the highest quality and were designed to operate alongside and interface with the finest digital synthesizers on the market. Input and output impedances are compatible with a wide variety of equipment. Modules that require trigger pulses can be activated by as little as a few millivolts or by as much as a 15-volt spike.

The book also contains foil patterns for etching circuit boards. Simple circuits can be wired on pre-etched boards that are available commercially, but more complex circuits work better and are easier to build with custom-etched boards. There are beginner etching kits at local electronic suppliers for those who have never had experience with etching.

I hope this book is a valuable addition to your electronic music library. The primary concern is to provide a useful reference for your journey through the ever-expanding world of electronic music synthesis.

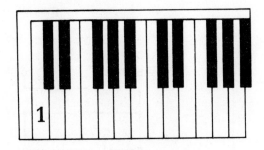

Power Supplies
and
Test Equipment

THIS BOOK CONTAINS MANY INTERESTING
and valuable synthesizer circuits, but you need first a power
supply. Because almost all designs require power, you must
build a unit that can deliver enough power to as many circuits as you care to build. Figure 1-1 is a schematic of a 15-
volt regulated single-ended power supply. All circuits in this
book that use linear ICs have been designed to operate with a
single-ended supply to avoid the necessity for the more
expensive bipolar design. Transformer T1 converts 110 volts
AC to 18 volts AC, while the bridge rectifier changes the AC
to pulsating DC. The capacitors C1 and C2 smooth out the DC
pulses and increase the voltage to 24 volts. Resistor R1 limits
current and voltage regulator IC1 maintains a steady 15-volt
output. Capacitor C3 serves as a final filter stage and potentiometer R2 provides an adjustable voltage output. The 24-volt
output, the 15-volt output, and the ground should all be connected to barrier strips to give easy access to circuits. All
parts for this, as well as the other circuits in this book, are
available at local electronic supply stores.

Current and voltage respond to resistance in quite a different manner. A 200-ohm resistor can significantly reduce

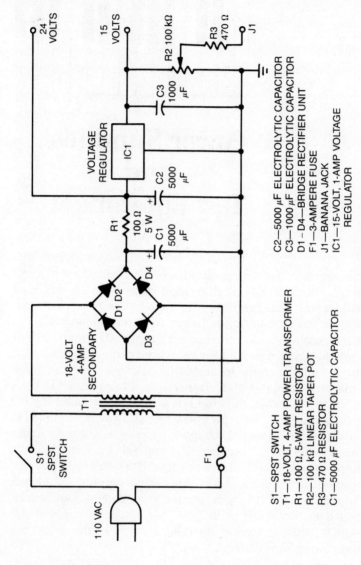

Fig. 1-1. A synthesizer power supply.

S1—SPST SWITCH
T1—18-VOLT, 4-AMP POWER TRANSFORMER
R1—100 Ω, 5-WATT RESISTOR
R2—100 kΩ LINEAR TAPER POT
R3—470 Ω RESISTOR
C1—5000 μF ELECTROLYTIC CAPACITOR

C2—5000 μF ELECTROLYTIC CAPACITOR
C3—1000 μF ELECTROLYTIC CAPACITOR
D1 – D4—BRIDGE RECTIFIER UNIT
F1—3-AMPERE FUSE
J1—BANANA JACK
IC1—15-VOLT, 1-AMP VOLTAGE
      REGULATOR

current flow, while a 68-kilohm resistor would reduce voltage by very little. Therefore to manually control voltage, one side of the potentiometer must be connected to ground. As in the schematic of Fig. 1-1, potentiometer R2 is connected to the 15-volt output on one side and to ground on the other, therefore enabling a sweep of the entire range of voltage from 0 to 15 volts.

Resistor R3 prevents the supply from shorting out in the event that R2 is adjusted to its highest setting and a wire from J1 inadvertently comes in contact with ground.

VOLTAGE DIVIDER

The control voltage range for all of the projects in this book is 0 to 15 volts. Some synthesizer systems use a 0- to 10-volt or 0- to 5-volt control range. Figure 1-2 shows a voltage divider that converts the 15-volt output to control 5- or 10-volt machines. Resistors R1, R2, and R3 are of equal value and thus divide the voltage into thirds. More elaborate voltage dividers are used in keyboards, and transistor biasing is also accomplished with dividers.

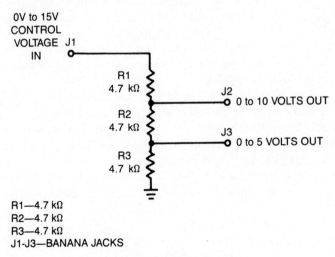

Fig. 1-2. A voltage divider.

VOLTAGE REGULATION

One of a synthesizer's main functions is to generate accurate pitches, a task that can only be accomplished with a rock-steady supply voltage. This requires the use of a voltage regulator, a device that produces a steady output even though its input might fluctuate. Most regulators are rated at only 1 ampere, so a full complement of circuits could put quite a strain on the device. One solution to this problem is to connect voltage-controlled amplifiers, preamps, mixers, ring modulators, reverbs, and other non-pitch-related circuits to the 24-volt output of the power supply. Make sure that all parts can handle the extra voltage before connecting them to the 24-volt supply. Circuits that must be connected to the 15-volt regulated supply are indicated in the schematic.

ABOUT CABLES AND CONNECTORS

Some synthesizer manufacturers use only audio cables to interconnect their circuits or *modules* as they are sometimes called. The designs in this book use two types of cables: the *audio* signals pass through shielded cable and mini-jacks, but *control voltages* and *pulses* pass through banana jacks, plugs, and unshielded cables. There are a number of reasons for this arrangement, not the least of which is economy. All audio signals must be routed via shielded cables and their corresponding plugs and jacks, which are more expensive.

Control voltages and pulses do not require shielding, so they can be routed through less expensive banana jacks and plugs. One other benefit from this system is that you then have a more easily traceable patching network due to color coding (black for control voltages, red for pulses, and grey shielded cable for audio). You'll need a wide variety of cable lengths to accommodate different distances between modules.

EQUIPMENT

Here are some of the things you must acquire if you intend to build any of the circuits in this book. You need a spool of solder and a soldering iron. If you intend to make your own circuit boards, you need direct-etching dry trans- fers, a bottle of etchant, and a board. Pre-etched boards are available, but make sure that the board will accommodate all parts and that the circuit is wired correctly. A multimeter comes in handy as does a transistor tester, and equip yourself with long-nose pliers, diagonal cutters, and wire strippers.

PART SUBSTITUTIONS

Most of the parts for projects were chosen on the basis of availability, but there are times when even common parts are hard to find. Bipolar transistors, both npn and pnp can be replaced by general purpose transistors of like polarity. Field-effect transistors present no problem, because almost any number can be substituted for any other of the same type. Capacitors can be substituted, but care must be taken to match the microfarad rating as close as possible or circuit performance will suffer. Power supply capacitors can vary to a great extent, but their voltage rating should exceed the sup- ply voltage by at least 10 volts.

All resistors are rated at $1/4$ watt unless otherwise noted. The rule for resistor substitution is that if other parts have been replaced, a different resistor value might be necessary. Experimentation is the key to success in electronic music synthesis, whether with different patches or different cir- cuits components.

CIRCUIT DESIGNER

This section explains how to construct a circuit designer, which provides a method of trying designs before actually soldering together the final circuit on the board. The designer provides the opportunity for you to try different parts, make design changes, and experiment with new designs. See Fig. 1-3.

First, a socket breadboard can be obtained from your local electronic supply house. The socket boards I use are two QT-35S sockets and a QT-35B bus strip. All sockets are formed from a prestressed, spring-loaded, noncorrosive

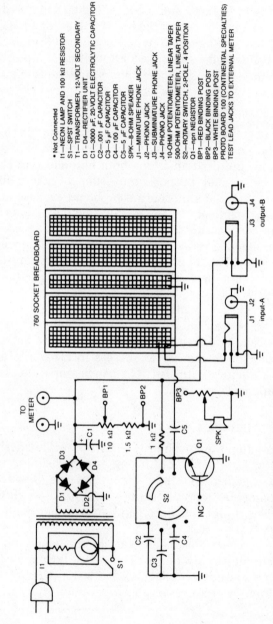

Fig. 1-3. A schematic of the circuit designer.

• Not Connected
I1—NEON LAMP AND 100 kΩ RESISTOR
S1—SPST SWITCH
T1—TRANSFORMER, 12-VOLT SECONDARY
D1 - D4—RECTIFIER UNIT
C1—3000 μF, 20-VOLT ELECTROLYTIC CAPACITOR
C2—.001 μF CAPACITOR
C3—5 μF CAPACITOR
C4—100 μF CAPACITOR
C5—5 μF CAPACITOR
SPK—8-OHM SPEAKER
J1—MINIATURE PHONE JACK
J2—PHONO JACK
J3—SUBMINIATURE PHONE JACK
J4—PHONO JACK
10-OHM POTENTIOMETER, LINEAR TAPER
500-OHM POTENTIOMETER, LINEAR TAPER
S2—ROTARY SWITCH, 2-POLE, 4 POSITION
Q1—npn NEGISTOR
BP1—RED BINDING POST
BP2—BLACK BINDING POST
BP3—WHITE BINDING POST
PROTO BOARD 100 (CONTINENTAL SPECIALTIES)
TEST LEAD JACKS TO EXTERNAL METER

nickel-silver alloy. Each socket has five tie points per terminal, and each bus strip has two separate rows of interconnect-
ing terminals. Boards conform to $^1/_{10}$-inch grid, are DIP
compatible, and will accommodate 10 flat-pack 14-lead ICs.

The cabinet of the designer is a 7-inch by 5-inch by 2-
inch metal chassis that houses all of the circuitry (Fig. 1-4).
The power supply is an unregulated 15-volt source that feeds
the bus terminals directly. An adjustable voltage divider
ranging from 3 to 15 volts is accessible through binding post
BP1. Test lead jacks facilitate meter monitoring during all circuit tests or operations.

A negistor oscillator is provided and generates pulse and
two audio frequencies for testing amplifiers, filters, or other
circuits (see Chapter 2). A small 8-ohm speaker is contained
within the unit for oscillator and low-power amplifier testing. A 500-ohm linear taper potentiometer serves not only as
a volume control for the speaker, but it can serve as a 500-
ohm line impedance output when the speaker is turned completely off.

A set of shielded jacks are incorporated to reduce hum
and noise when the unit used with external equipment. Jack
J1 is a miniature phone jack, J3 is a subminiature phone jack,
and J2 and J4 are RCA jacks.

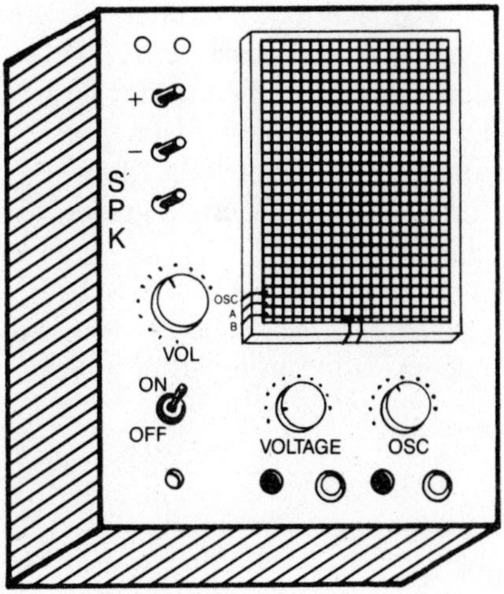

Fig. 1-4. Pictorial diagram
of circuit designer.

TRANSISTOR TESTER

A very simple transistor tester can be constructed from just a handful of parts, as Fig. 1-5 illustrates. Battery B1 is a common transistor radio 9-volt type that is connected to polarity-reversing switch S1. When a transistor is placed in socket J1 or connected by the alligator clips and switch S2 is pressed, diode D1 should light up. If this does not happen, switch S1 to the opposite position and again press switch S2. If there is still no light from D1, the transistor is not good. If diode D1 glows when switch S2 is not pressed, then the transistor is also not good. Diode D1 glows red for pnp transistors and green for npn. This unit can test power transistors as well as low level transistors.

UNIJUNCTION TESTER

Bipolar and field-effect transistors do not actually pass the input through; instead, the input at the base controls the impedance between the collector and the emitter. This isolates different circuit functions and prevents undesirable interaction. However, the unijunction transistor and the PUT transistor (programmable unijunction transistor) are exceptions. Figure 1-6 is a circuit designed to test unijunction transistors.

Capacitor C1 is charged through resistor R1. When it reaches approximately 1.7 volts, the normally high impedance between the emitter and base 2 changes to a very low impedance, which discharges C1 through diode D1. Once the capacitor has been discharged, the impedance between the emitter and base 2 goes high and capacitor C1 starts to charge again.

The flash rate of LED D1 is about two per second. The circuit can easily be breadboarded, so it is not absolutely necessary to put together a permanent test unit.

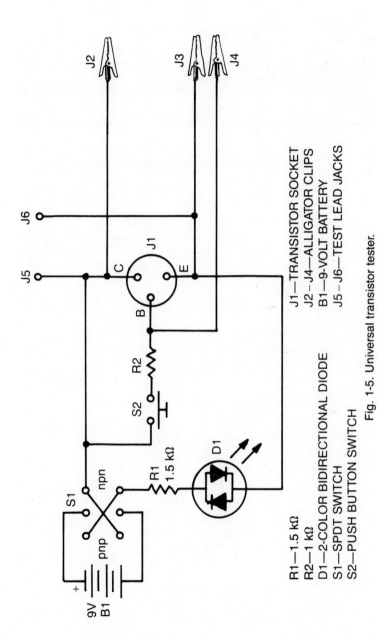

Fig. 1-5. Universal transistor tester.

J1—TRANSISTOR SOCKET
J2 – J4—ALLIGATOR CLIPS
B1—9-VOLT BATTERY
J5 – J6—TEST LEAD JACKS

R1—1.5 kΩ
R2—1 kΩ
D1—2-COLOR BIDIRECTIONAL DIODE
S1—SPDT SWITCH
S2—PUSH BUTTON SWITCH

9

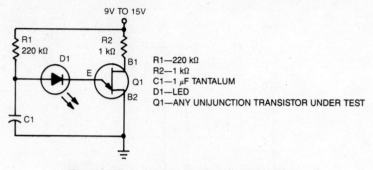

Fig. 1-6. Test circuit for unijunction transistors.

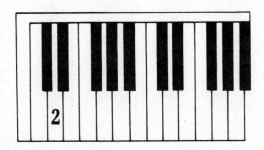

Sources

CHAPTER 1 INTRODUCED THE UNIJUNCTION transistor and the programmable unijunction transistor. These devices have been around since the first commercial synthesizers, and there is still no better way of generating a sawtooth wave.

The most important waveshape in electronic music is the sawtooth because it contains both odd and even harmonics and can easily be converted to other waveshapes. However, it is very difficult to convert other waveshapes to a sawtooth.

Square waves produce only odd harmonics. A 50 percent duty cycle, as in Fig. 2-1, sounds very much like a clarinet. Changing the pulse width (duty cycle) with a control voltage can produce very interesting tonalities.

Triangular waves can be generated by running the square wave through an integrater, such as the one described in Chapter 9. Like square waves, odd harmonics are the only product of triangular waves, but their intensity is considerably diminished.

Sine waves contain no harmonics at all and are more useful as low-frequency control voltages or as a very low frequency audio source.

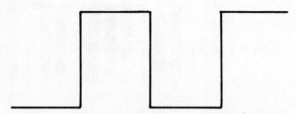

Fig. 2-1. A 50 percent pulse width waveshape.

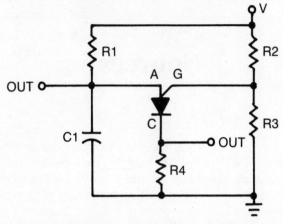

Fig. 2-2. Programmable unijunction transistor circuit.

Fig. 2-3. Unijunction transistor waveshape.

In Fig. 2-2, capacitor C1 is charged through resistor R1. When the voltage exceeds that established by voltage divider R2 and R3, then the gate turns the transistor on and C1 discharges through R4, producing a needle pulse at the cathode lead of the transistor. The sawtooth wave is taken from the anode of the transistor, however an oscilloscope reveals that the waveshape is actually a reverse exponential curve, as Fig. 2-3 illustrates.

NEGISTORS

It would appear that generating a linear sawtooth could best be accomplished with the use of a conventional bipolar transistor. When their emitter and collector leads are reversed, as in Fig. 2-4, bipolar transistors exhibit an amazing characteristic known as *negative resistance*. Capacitor C1 charges through resistor R1 and potentiometer R2, and when at a certain voltage, the transistor's junction resistance breaks down and C1 discharges.

The oscillator is stable and the sawtooth wave is linear, but pitch range is somewhat less than the five-octave range required of a professional source oscillator. The negistor's range can be extended by increasing the supply voltage. There is a 24-volt tap available (see Chapter 1, Fig. 1-1), but it is unregulated and pitch integrity will inevitably suffer.

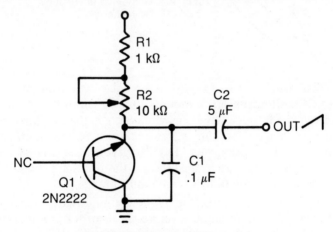

Fig. 2-4. Negistor oscillator circuit.

UNIJUNCTION OSCILLATOR

Because of its stability and wide range, the unijunction transistor is ideally suited to the job of source wave generation except for its exponential waveshape. Since the unijunction was born out of research with field-effect principals, adding a field-effect transistor can solve the problem. Compare Fig. 2-2 with Fig. 2-5. The latter shows the exponential response curve of an FET transistor. When combined with the unijunction waveshape of Fig. 2.2 as in Fig. 2-6, they cancel each other and produce a straight ramp.

Fig. 2-5. FET transistor exponential response curve.

Fig. 2-6. Combined unijunction and FET waveshapes.

The oscillator in Fig. 2-7 is a wide-range, high-quality unit. Potentiometer R1 is mounted on the circuit board and controls the frequency when switch S1 is in manual position (position shown). When it is in the external position, an external control voltage (CV IN) is engaged. Resistors R1 and R2 bias transistor Q1 to ensure that the oscillator responds evenly to the entire 0- to 15-volt control range.

Transistor Q2 facilitates frequency modulation through capacitor C1 and potentiometer R6. Resistor R4 prevents the oscillator from cutting out when the control voltage goes to zero, and R5 keeps the oscillator from latching when a 15-volt control level is reached. Transistor Q3 is the generating element and switch S2 acts as a high or low range selector. Capacitor C3 is the low range while C2 handles the high, with plenty of overlap and more than ten octaves of overall range. The reverse exponential output of transistor Q3 is passed to FETs Q5 and Q6, which straighten the waveshape and prepare the signal for further processing and output.

14

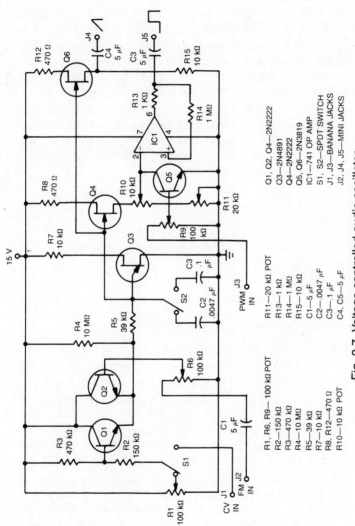

Fig. 2-7. Voltage-controlled audio oscillator.

R1, R6, R9—100 kΩ POT
R2—150 kΩ
R3—470 kΩ
R4—10 MΩ
R5—39 kΩ
R7—10 kΩ
R8, R12—470 Ω
R10—10 kΩ POT

R11—20 kΩ POT
R13—1 kΩ
R14—1 MΩ
R15—10 kΩ
C1—5 μF
C2—.0047 μF
C3—1 μF
C4, C5—5 μF

Q1, Q2, Q4—2N2222
Q3—2N4891
Q4—2N2222
Q5, Q6—2N3819
IC1—741 OP AMP
S1, S2—SPDT SWITCH
J1, J3—BANANA JACKS
J2, J4, J5—MINI JACKS

15

Integrated circuit IC1 serves as a Schmitt trigger (square wave converter); potentiometer R10 determines the pulse width and R11 functions as a trimmer. Resistor R14 should be omitted until the oscillator is tested. To test, connect the oscillator to a 15-volt power supply, connect the square wave output to an audio amplifier, adjust potentiometer R10 to the minimum or ground side, and then adjust R11 until the sound almost cuts out. This should equal approximately a 5 percent duty cycle as shown in Fig. 2-8. If the integrated circuit malfunctions, then install resistor R14. Transistor Q4 provides a means of modulating the pulse width by an external control voltage. Figure 2-9 shows the foil pattern layout for the VCO circuit of Fig. 2-7.

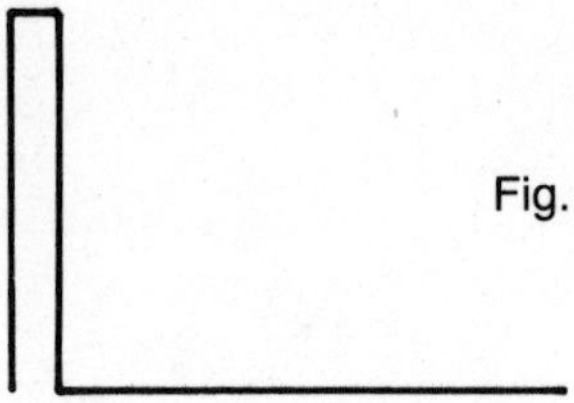

Fig. 2-8. A 5-percent-pulse-width waveshape.

LOW-FREQUENCY OSCILLATOR

In the production of electronic music, there often arises the need to slowly modulate frequency, amplitude, or filtering. This is the job of the low-frequency oscillator.

In the schematic of Fig. 2-10, switch S1 determines the overall range while potentiometer R7 controls the frequency. Resistors R6 and R8 keep the oscillator from cutting out due to too much or too little voltage. A triangular wave is generated at pin 4 of IC1 but it is not of sufficient amplitude to function as a control voltage, so transistor Q1 amplifies the signal to a useful level. The range of the oscillator is very wide and can serve as a source of high-frequency modulation as well as low. Resistor R7 is the only control that is mounted on the circuit board (Fig. 2-11), and resistors R1 through R4 are mounted on switch S1, a three-pole four-position rotary switch.

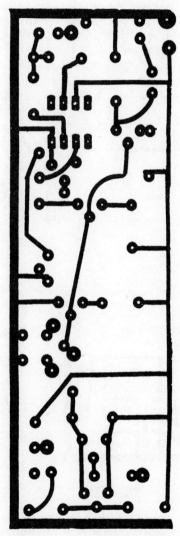

Fig. 2-9. Foil pattern for voltage-controlled oscillator.

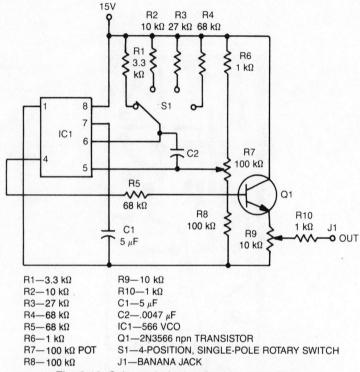

Fig. 2-10. Schematic for low-frequency oscillator.

R1—3.3 kΩ	R9—10 kΩ
R2—10 kΩ	R10—1 kΩ
R3—27 kΩ	C1—5 μF
R4—68 kΩ	C2—.0047 μF
R5—68 kΩ	IC1—566 VCO
R6—1 kΩ	Q1—2N3566 npn TRANSISTOR
R7—100 kΩ POT	S1—4-POSITION, SINGLE-POLE ROTARY SWITCH
R8—100 kΩ	J1—BANANA JACK

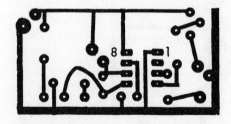

Fig. 2-11. Foil pattern for low-frequency oscillator.

WHITE NOISE GENERATOR

White noise is the result of all audio frequencies being reproduced at the same time and at the same amplitude. At first this might seem like quite a task for one circuit to perform, but as the schematic of Fig. 2-12 shows, it is just a simple two-transistor circuit.

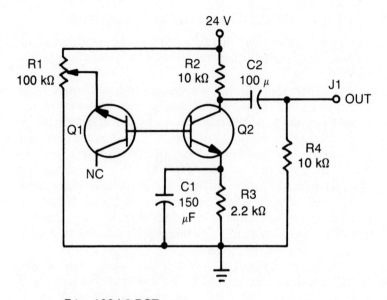

Fig. 2-12. Schematic for white noise generator.

R1—100 kΩ POT
R2—10 kΩ
R3—2.2 kΩ
R4—10 kΩ
C1—150 μF
C2—100 μF
Q1—2N2222
Q2—2N3565
J1—MINI JACK

Transistor Q2 functions as a preamplifier with its base connected to a transistor in the random avalanche mode. Transistor Q1 looks somewhat like the negistor in Fig. 2-2, but because the base lead is used instead of the collector and there are no frequency-selecting components, a cascade of random frequencies is generated. The prototype noise generator was built on a pre-etched and drilled general-purpose circuit board. Potentiometer R1 is a board-mounted trimmer that should be adjusted for maximum audio output.

VOLTAGE-CONTROLLED PULSE GENERATOR

Many of the functions of a synthesizer are initiated by pulses, so a sophisticated pulse clock is absolutely necessary.

The time-keeping duties are given to a 4001 quad NOR gate. In Fig. 2-13, transistor Q1 controls the frequency with a voltage applied to jack J1 or manually by potentiometer R4. A six-position rotary switch provides an overall range from one pulse every 20 seconds to several thousand pulses per second. The generator was designed to drive the sequencer described in Chapter 6, so interfacing facilities have been maximized. The most obvious interface is the control of the pulse speed by the sequencer. Another important function is the single pulse, which greatly simplifies tuning by advancing the sequencer just one stage.

Referring to Fig. 2-13, switch S3 engages the single-pulse mode by accessing the bounceless switch circuit consisting of a NOR gate, resistor R5, capacitor C7, and switch S2 (a momentary contact push button switch). Once tuning has been completed, switch S3 can be changed to the "up" position for pulsing. In the "stop start" mode, the generator stops when a high-level pulse appears at jack J4 and will remain stopped as long as the signal at J4 stays high or until the "manual start" switch S4 is pressed.

Jacks J2 and J3 provide an alternating pulse output for positional effects or double-note production. Note that when LED D1 is on, the jack connected to it (J2) measures a low (0 volts). Simultaneously, D2 is off, but J3 is then high. Therefore, when preparing the board layout, locate J2 next to or under LED D2 so that when D2 is on, you get a high output at J2. The same goes with J3 and D1. This scheme might seem contradictory, but it is designed this way to avoid undue strain and possible damage to IC2.

If the foil pattern in Fig. 2-14 seems inadequate to support all of the circuitry, it's because many parts are mounted to switches or jacks. For example, all capacitors connected to switch S1 are mounted on a two-pole, six-position switch. Potentiometer R4 is the only control that is mounted directly onto the circuit board.

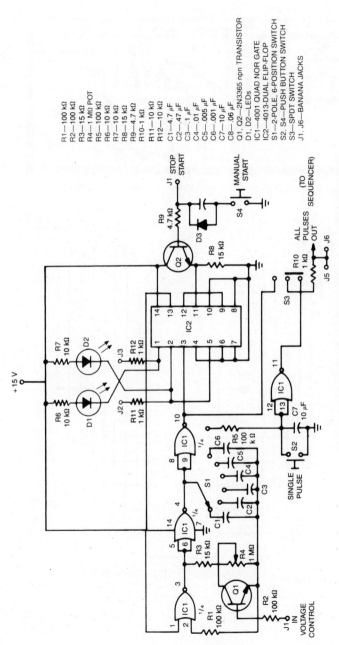

Fig. 2-13. Voltage-controlled pulse generator schematic.

R1—100 kΩ
R2—100 kΩ
R3—15 kΩ
R4—1 MΩ POT
R5—100 kΩ
R6—10 kΩ
R7—10 kΩ
R8—15 kΩ
R9—4.7 kΩ
R10—1 kΩ
R11—10 kΩ
R12—10 kΩ
C1—4.7 μF
C2—47 μF
C3—1 μF
C4—01 μF
C5—005 μF
C6—001 μF
C7—10 μF
C8—06 μF
Q1, Q2—2N3365 npn TRANSISTOR
D1, D2—LEDs
IC1—4001 QUAD NOR GATE
IC2—4013-DUAL FLIP-FLOP
S1—2-POLE, 6-POSITION SWITCH
S2, S4—PUSH BUTTON SWITCH
S3—SPDT SWITCH
J1, J6—BANANA JACKS

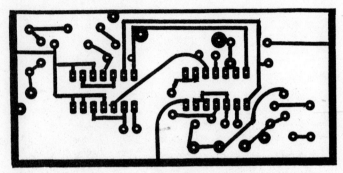

Fig. 2-14. Foil pattern for voltage-controlled pulse generator.

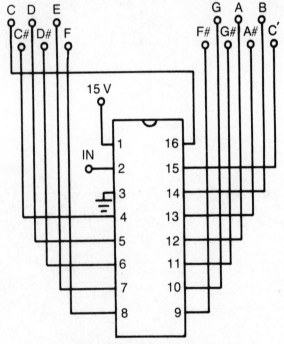

Fig. 2-15. Note layout for top-octave generator.

TOP-OCTAVE GENERATOR

One of the most interesting devices to come out of digital research is an item called a *top-octave generator*. This integrated circuit receives a square wave input at pin 2 and divides the frequency into 13 equally tempered diatonic tones. The tones are then sent to a gating keyboard like that used with the small system in Chapter 10.

The parts numbers I used for this unit are 50240 or Mostek MK 5083 and they can be obtained through the larger mail-order supplier. Figure 2-15 shows the pin layout of the top octave circuit, and Fig. 2-16 is a block diagram of a system for generating three full octaves of square waves.

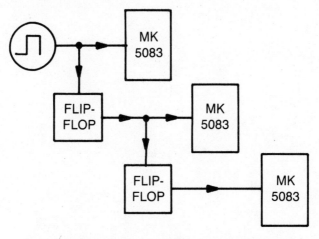

Fig. 2-16. Block diagram for three-octave synthesizer.

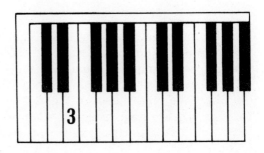

Filters

ALL SOUND WAVES (EXCEPT SINE WAVES) contain harmonics that are generated at the same time as the primary frequency, but they are higher in pitch and lower in volume. It is the presence or absence of these harmonics that determine the kind of sound an instrument can produce.

No area of synthesis lends itself more readily to experimentation than the manipulation of harmonics. Try running a signal through coils, transformers, diodes, or combinations of components—whatever combination you like to make it sound unique, unusual, or just plain good.

Filters that are used in music synthesizers are classified (for the most part) in one of four categories. A first-order filter is 6 dB per octave, which means that for every octave beyond the cutoff point, an additional 6 decibels of volume reduction takes place. The same applies to second-order (12 dB per octave), third-order (18 dB per octave), and fourth-order (24 dB per octave) filters.

The time-constant characteristic of capacitors is used to alter the tonal quality of audio sources. Small capacitors charge quickly and consequently cannot respond to the slow charging rate of low-frequency audio signals. A single capac-itor by itself does not make a good filter because it is unstable with respect to amplitude and frequency. Adding a resistor gives the needed stability and maximizes the effectiveness of the filter. The type shown in Fig. 3-1 is a *high-pass* filter because only low frequencies are attenuated. Simply revers-ing the position of the two components achieves the opposite effect, or *low pass*, as in Fig. 3-2. These filters use both a series component and a ground leg; therefore, they are called *two-pole filters*. The schematic in Fig. 3-3 utilizes high-and low-pass elements in a two-stage, 12-position *bandpass* for-mat filter. Switch S1 selects the amount of filtering to take place by feeding the input to one of five differently rated capacitors. An adjustable ground leg is provided by resistors R6 and R7. The signal then passes on to the low-pass section where one of five different resistor/capacitor combinations is selected. This filter controls the overall bandwidth of applied signals and has proven to be a very useful manual control sys-tem.

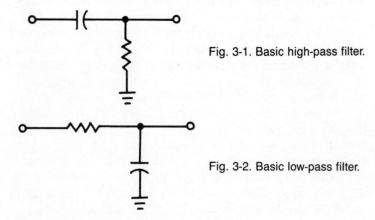

Fig. 3-1. Basic high-pass filter.

Fig. 3-2. Basic low-pass filter.

VOLTAGE-CONTROLLED FILTERS

The voltage control techniques used with VCOs can be used to vary the amount of filtering. Three types explained here are high-pass, low-pass, and resonant voltage-con-trolled filters.

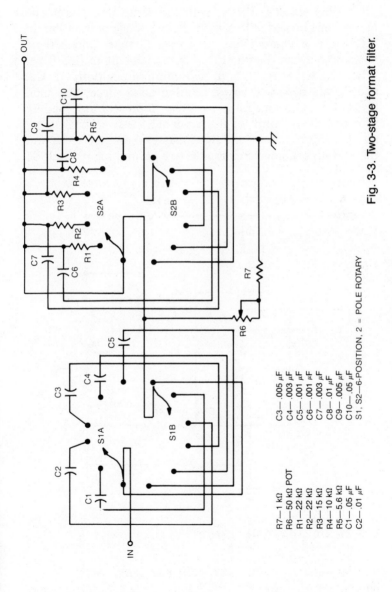

Fig. 3-3. Two-stage format filter.

R7—1 kΩ
R6—50 kΩ POT
R1—22 kΩ
R2—22 kΩ
R3—15 kΩ
R4—10 kΩ
R5—5.6 kΩ
C1—.05 μF
C2—.01 μF

C3—.005 μF
C4—.003 μF
C5—.001 μF
C6—.001 μF
C7—.003 μF
C8—.01 μF
C9—.005 μF
C10—.05 μF
S1, S2—6-POSITION, 2 = POLE ROTARY

HIGH PASS

With high-pass filters, both the series and shunt elements must be varied to exploit the full range of the filter. In Fig. 3-4, the combination of a potentiometer and a fixed resistor facilitate the control of both elements of this filter. When the wiper of R5 is in its minimum position, C1, C2, and C3 are bypassed so no filtering takes place. The total resistance of R5 and R6 is too great to present any loading problems at the input. As the wiper of R5 is swept to is maximum position, more of the signal passes through C1, C2, and C3, and R6 becomes a more effective ground leg. Switch S1

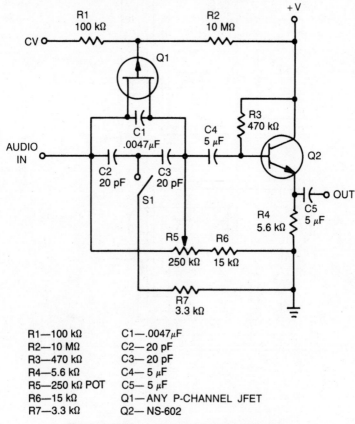

R1—100 kΩ	C1—.0047µF
R2—10 MΩ	C2— 20 pF
R3—470 kΩ	C3— 20 pF
R4—5.6 kΩ	C4— 5 µF
R5—250 kΩ POT	C5— 5 µF
R6—15 kΩ	Q1—ANY P-CHANNEL JFET
R7—3.3 kΩ	Q2— NS-602

Fig. 3-4. Voltage-controlled high-pass filter.

permits changing the cutoff point by 2 octaves, a very useful feature. Transistor Q1 performs the control-voltage processing duties, but take note that potentiometer R5 is an override control and determines the depth of the filtering. A dual purpose is served by Q2: It amplifies to compensate for signal loss due to filtering and it isolates to eliminate loading. Despite the simplicity of this second-order filter, it is effective, versatile, and can be operated manually or with a control voltage.

LOW PASS

The low-pass filter is a simpler design because you need only to vary the ground leg of the filter. In Fig. 3-5, resistor R1 and capacitor C1 are the filtering elements in this design.

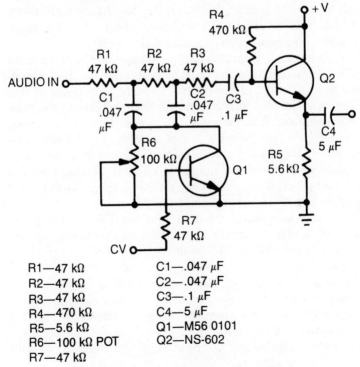

R1—47 kΩ	C1—.047 μF
R2—47 kΩ	C2—.047 μF
R3—47 kΩ	C3—.1 μF
R4—470 kΩ	C4—5 μF
R5—5.6 kΩ	Q1—M56 0101
R6—100 kΩ POT	Q2—NS-602
R7—47 kΩ	

Fig. 3-5. Voltage-controlled low-pass filter.

But by adding two more filter elements, R2 and C2, a more pronounced effect and sharper response curve can be obtained. Potentiometer R6 is the manual control, while transistor Q1 handles the control voltage. Transistor Q2 amplifies and isolates the filter from loading effects. The cutoff frequency of this filter is approximately 200 hertz, making this a very dynamic filter and a valuable addition to any synthesizer system.

RESONANT FILTER

A resonant filter differs from the filters discussed thus far in that the signal is amplified to the point of resonance (where just one frequency is emphasized). Figure 3-6 shows such a filter using a 741 op amp, which requires biasing for a single-ended power supply (foil pattern in Fig. 3-7). Resistors R1 and R2 accomplish this rather handily. Potentiometer R3 controls the depth of the filter's effect, while R9 determines what frequency is accentuated.

Transistor Q1 applies control voltage, but keep in mind that R9 is an override and must be in its open position to realize the full effect of the control voltage. The nature of this filter is some what volatile, so care must be taken or the filter will oscillate. Potentiometer R3 is the depth control and should be set to the position of minimum resistance. The control voltage could also be a source of overdrive, so potentiometer R7 provides a means to tailor this voltage for the desired effect. If these rules are followed, there should be no problems with the operation of this filter.

The type of sound obtained from this filter classifies it as a fourth-order bandpass with a 24-decibel-per-octave response curve. All of this means that the filter can produce the kind of sounds that can be described as "fat" or "wet." These sounds are very interesting when used with a sequencer and white noise generator to produce super percussion simulation. An alternate design is shown in Fig. 3-8 (foil pattern in Fig. 3-9). The high-pass and low-pass functions are separated and can be controlled through S1 or with two different voltages.

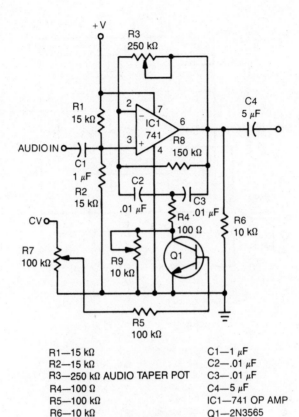

R1—15 kΩ
R2—15 kΩ
R3—250 kΩ AUDIO TAPER POT
R4—100 Ω
R5—100 kΩ
R6—10 kΩ
R7—100 kΩ LINEAR TAPER POT
R8—150 kΩ
R9—10 kΩ LINEAR POT

C1—1 µF
C2—.01 µF
C3—.01 µF
C4—5 µF
IC1—741 OP AMP
Q1—2N3565

Fig. 3-6. Voltage-controlled resonant filter.

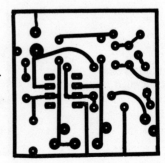

Fig. 3-7. Foil pattern for voltage-controlled resonant filter.

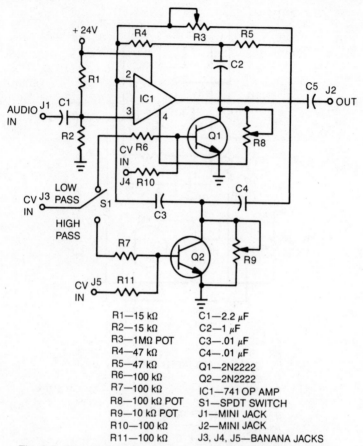

R1—15 kΩ
R2—15 kΩ
R3—1MΩ POT
R4—47 kΩ
R5—47 kΩ
R6—100 kΩ
R7—100 kΩ
R8—100 kΩ POT
R9—10 kΩ POT
R10—100 kΩ
R11—100 kΩ

C1—2.2 μF
C2—1 μF
C3—.01 μF
C4—.01 μF
Q1—2N2222
Q2—2N2222
IC1—741 OP AMP
S1—SPDT SWITCH
J1—MINI JACK
J2—MINI JACK
J3, J4, J5—BANANA JACKS

Fig. 3-8. Alternate design for voltage-controlled resonant filter.

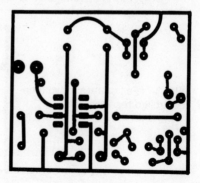

Fig. 3-9. Foil pattern for the alternate voltage-controlled resonant filter.

VOICING CIRCUITS

There are many other types of filters—parametric, graphic, band reject, etc.—but some interesting tonalities can be achieved with the use of passive voicing circuits. Figure 3-10 shows a prime example of this type of filter. Sometimes the effect is intensified when used with another filter or another waveshape. Some very odd waveshapes can be obtained with the use of a voicing circuit despite its simplicity.

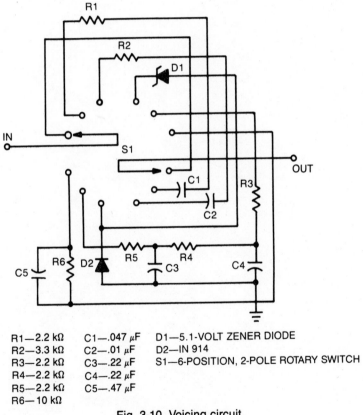

R1—2.2 kΩ	C1—.047 μF	D1—5.1-VOLT ZENER DIODE
R2—3.3 kΩ	C2—.01 μF	D2—IN 914
R3—2.2 kΩ	C3—.22 μF	S1—6-POSITION, 2-POLE ROTARY SWITCH
R4—2.2 kΩ	C4—.22 μF	
R5—2.2 kΩ	C5—.47 μF	
R6—10 kΩ		

Fig. 3-10. Voicing circuit.

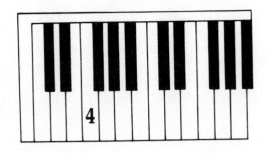

Amplifiers

ALL STUDIOS REQUIRE AN AMPLIFIER TO drive the speakers, and it should be powerful enough to deliver a strong, clean, undistored sound. Amplifiers must contend with a wide variety of inputs, so when selecting a studio unit, make sure it can handle present as well as potential expansion needs.

Amplifiers provide a means of increasing the amplitude of a signal that is too low for practical application. Professional studio amplifiers are powerful enough to drive several speaker systems. If you intend to build your own studio, you should select an amplifier with enough power to fill the room with a rather high level of undistorted sound. (More information is in Chapter 10, Systems Planning.)

PREAMP

Preamplifiers are used to process sounds that are generated by external sources such as a microphone, electric guitar, etc., but the signal might not be of adequate amplitude. In these cases, you need a preamplifier like the one illustrated in Fig. 4-1. Capacitor C1 of this design decouples the input and feeds it to potentiometer R1, which is both a volume control and reverse-biasing resistor for transistor Q1. Resistor R2 is the ground reference and discharge path for the output decoupling capacitor C2. As simple as this circuit is, it should meet all your preamplifier needs.

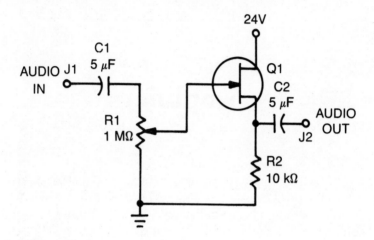

R1—1 MΩ POT
R2—10 kΩ
C1—5 µF
C2—5 µF
Q1—B5-170 FET TRANSISTOR, N-CHANNEL
J1, J2—MINI JACKS

Fig. 4-1. Preamplifier schematic.

VOLTAGE-CONTROLLED AMPLIFIER

All sound sources of synthesizers produce a continuous output and therefore must be amplitude modulated by a voltage-controlled amplifier (VCA). Figure 4-2 shows a design with a somewhat unusual signal-shunting approach to amplitude control.

Referring to the figure, audio enters at J1 and passes through decoupling capacitor C1. Potentiometer R1 controls

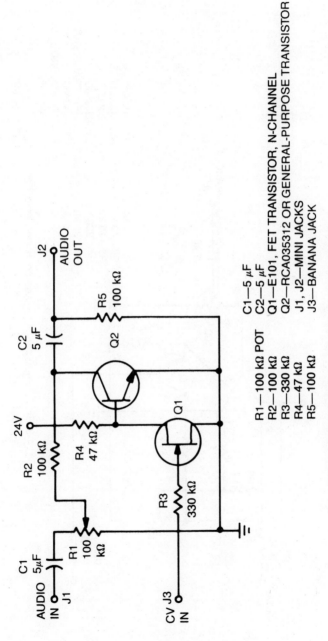

Fig. 4-2. Schematic for voltage-controlled amplifier.

C1—5 µF
C2—5 µF
Q1—E101, FET TRANSISTOR, N-CHANNEL
Q2—RCA035312 OR GENERAL-PURPOSE TRANSISTOR
J1, J2—MINI JACKS
J3—BANANA JACK

R1—100 kΩ POT
R2—100 kΩ
R3—330 kΩ
R4—47 kΩ
R5—100 kΩ

37

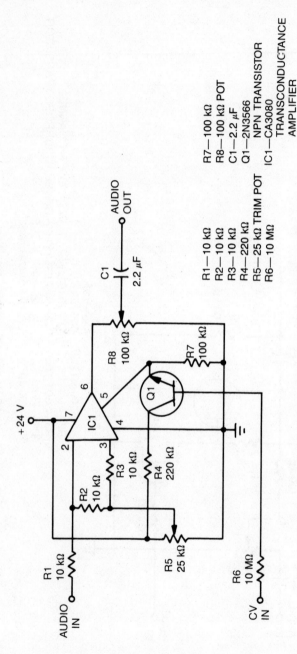

Fig. 4-3. Transconductance voltage-controlled amplifier.

R1—10 kΩ
R2—10 kΩ
R3—10 kΩ
R4—220 kΩ
R5—25 kΩ TRIM POT
R6—10 MΩ

R7—100 kΩ
R8—100 kΩ POT
C1—2.2 μF
Q1—2N3566
NPN TRANSISTOR
IC1—CA3080
TRANSCONDUCTANCE
AMPLIFIER

the overall volume, while resistor R2 prevents circuit loading. Transistor Q2 is normally biased on and consequently shunts the signal to ground. When a control voltage is applied to transistor Q1 through resistor R3, transistor Q2 turns off and the signal passes to the output.

Since this design is not actually an amplifier, it in no way alters or modifies the frequency response characteristic of the input. Because of the nature of this design, signal leakage is not possible, nor is there a problem with DC "thump" due to an inherent flaw in transistors called *overshooting*.

Another design is included here because of its use of the extremely popular CA3080 transconductance amplifier. When a control voltage is applied to the CA3080 through R3, it passes the input to pin 6. The CA3080 can be somewhat temperamental and sometimes presents difficulties, so an extremely stable design is provided in Fig. 4-3. The foil pattern is in Fig. 4-4.

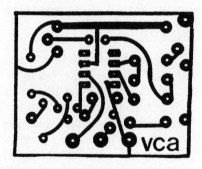

Fig. 4-4. Foil pattern for transconductance voltage-controlled amplifier.

A design using an optocoupler is shown in Fig. 4-5. Resistor R3 is selected by running a high level signal through the unit and trying different values until you hear nothing. Do not use a resistor smaller than 1000 ohms, in fact it is advisable to use the largest value which will still result in zero output.

The sources for control voltages to operate these VCAs is almost endless—sequencers, LFOs, envelope detectors, and the most common and versatile unit, the envelope generator. A full discussion of envelope generation is undertaken in the next chapter.

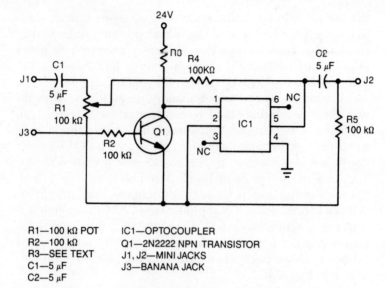

R1—100 kΩ POT   IC1—OPTOCOUPLER
R2—100 kΩ   Q1—2N2222 NPN TRANSISTOR
R3—SEE TEXT   J1, J2—MINI JACKS
C1—5 μF   J3—BANANA JACK
C2—5 μF

Fig. 4-5. Optocoupled voltage-controlled amplifier.

MIXERS

To produce more than one sound at a time requires the use of a mixer. Figure 4-6 is the schematic of a four-input unit that should meet all of your mixing needs. Capacitors C1 through C4 pass the inputs along to potentiometers R1 through R4 respectively. Resistors R5 through R8 provide isolation for the inputs and pass the signal along to the decoupling capacitor C5. Resistor R10 reverse biases transistor Q1, which amplifies the signal to compensate for losses due to the resistor network. If a stereo output is necessary, then just build two units.

Because all of the inputs are combined, a single envelope, as shown in Fig. 4-7, can be used to generate complex tonalities.

SPEAKERS

Speakers come in many different sizes, shapes, and styles, but when it comes to studio monitors, the only consideration is quality. Every studio should have one pair of

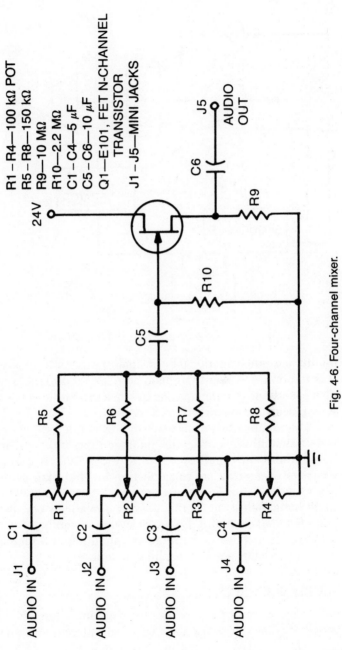

R1 – R4—100 kΩ POT
R5 – R8—150 kΩ
R9—10 MΩ
R10—2.2 MΩ
C1 – C4—5 µF
C5 – C6—10 µF
Q1—E101, FET N-CHANNEL
TRANSISTOR
J1 –J5—MINI JACKS

Fig. 4-6. Four-channel mixer.

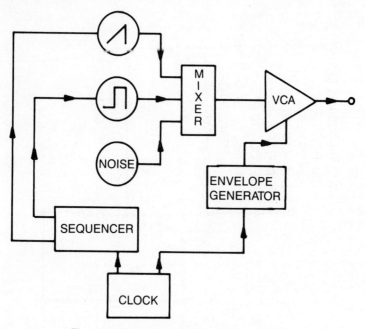

Fig. 4-7. Common envelope block diagram.

quality monitors and one pair of small inexpensive speakers. It is important to hear the music over several different types of speakers and different rooms because the studio is not the only place your music will be heard.

The compensation network of Fig. 4-8 allows speaker system switching. Connect the main monitors to the system A outputs and the small speakers to the system B outputs. Resistors R1 and R2 act as protection for the small system. These and resistors R3 and R4 are from 2 to 10 ohms at 10 or more watts. Select values that provide a relatively consistent volume when switching from one system to another. System C can be located in another room and should follow the same rules for resistor selection as the B system.

AMBIENCE RECOVERY SYSTEM

When a symphony orchestra plays in a concert hall, much of what you hear comes from behind you. Waveshape

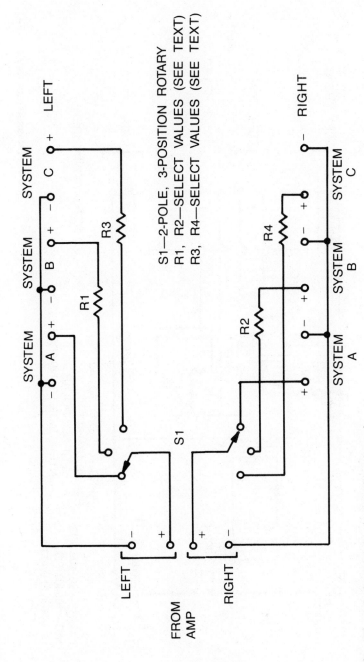

Fig. 4-8. Speaker compensation network.

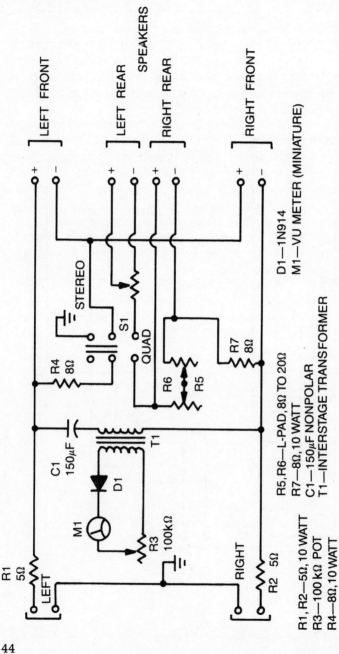

Fig. 4-9. Ambience recovery system.

SPEAKERS

LEFT FRONT

LEFT REAR

RIGHT REAR

RIGHT FRONT

STEREO

QUAD

S1

R4
8Ω

C1
150µF

D1

M1

R3
100kΩ

R5 R6

R7
8Ω

T1

R1
5Ω

LEFT

R2 5Ω

RIGHT

R1, R2—5Ω, 10 WATT
R3—100 KΩ POT
R4—8Ω, 10 WATT
R5, R6—L-PAD, 8Ω TO 20Ω
R7—8Ω, 10 WATT
C1—150µF NONPOLAR
T1—INTERSTAGE TRANSFORMER
D1—1N914
M1—VU METER (MINIATURE)

44

reinforcement, cancellation effects, and natural echo are the elements that make a concert exciting. Listening to a record of a symphony on a two-speaker system does not have the same impact because all of the sonic information is collected on only two tracks and is presented in front of you (usually). The room you are in cannot duplicate the phase relationships encountered in a concert hall.

It is possible to recover much of the ambience of the concert hall by adding two extra speakers and utilizing the unit in Fig. 4-9. The sound coming from the rear via the two extra speakers is equal to the sum and the difference of the front channels. The sum and difference is a close approximation of the natural reinforcement and cancellation effects that occur behind you in a concert hall, so this can achieve a very realistic simulation. The natural echo that was recorded on the "front" tracks can now also be reproduced from the rear to further enhance the illusion.

In the schematic, meter M1 deflects only when there is a stereo signal present to indicate a processable signal. Potentiometers R5 and R6 act as multisection controls for easily coordinated adjustment. Transformer T1 should have no less than a 1000-ohm primary.

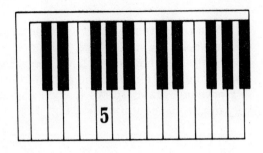

Envelopes

THE TECHNIQUES IN THIS CHAPTER PRESENT an awesome control unit that can facilitate the creation of sounds that exist nowhere else. These complex waveforms can be digitally sampled and stored, thus enabling the user to acquire a personal library of sounds. Remember that the key to success with this envelope-generating module is experimentation.

All synthesizers must provide a means by which to control the amplitude of the music. The voltage-controlled amplifier does just that, with the aid of control pulses produced by keyboards, sequencers, etc. These devices however, for the most part, generate only step voltages that just switch the amplifier on or off.

Enter the *envelope generator*, or *function generator* as it is sometimes called. Early versions of this device were known as ASD units; they allowed the user to control the attack (time it takes to rise to full volume), sustain (amount of time it remains at full volume), and decay (time required for the volume to return to fully off). Then came the ADSR, or attack, decay, sustain, and release, and when even more stages were added, this module became one of the most confusing and difficult to operate. To add insult to injury, once adjusted, you were confined to only that volume contour.

With the advent of digital synthesizers, envelopes have become complex multi-stage monsters, and all hopes for user-controlled envelopes have been abandoned. If this weren't enough, close examination of the digital synthesizer's envelope graph shows that all elements are linear—a very unmusical condition (see Fig. 5-1).

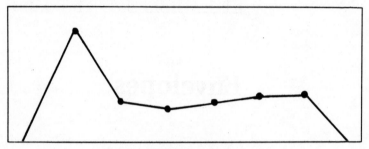

Fig. 5-1. Digital envelope graph.

A choice module would have the following attributes.

- The capability of producing linear and exponential output
- Manual or automatic input response
- Ability to instantaneously change envelope contour
- Must be programmable for complex multistage envelopes

The envelope generator described in this chapter can do all of these things and more. In the schematic of Fig. 5-2, use S1 to select the manual or automatic function. In manual mode, the attack and sustain times are determined by the pulse from a keyboard or other manually operated device. In the automatic mode, the attack and sustain times are preset so they are independent of the input pulse width. The 555 timer (IC1) isolates the input pulse and provides a fixed operating pulse, thus facilitating a wide range of trigger sensitivity (from a few millivolts to 15 volts).

Transistor Q1 supplies the necessary negative trigger to IC1 while Q2 prevents interaction between the attack and sustain by not allowing the sustain timing capacitor to charge

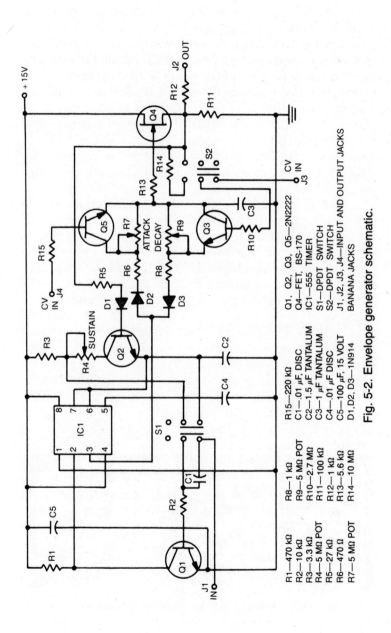

Fig. 5-2. Envelope generator schematic.

R1—470 kΩ
R2—10 kΩ
R3—3.3 kΩ
R4—5 MΩ POT
R5—27 kΩ
R6—470 Ω
R7—5 MΩ POT

R8—1 kΩ
R9—5 MΩ POT
R10—2.7 MΩ
R11—100 kΩ
R12—1 kΩ
R13—5.6 kΩ
R14—10 MΩ

R15—220 kΩ
C1—.01 μF, DISC
C2—1.5 μF TANTALUM
C3—1 μF TANTALUM
C4—.01 μF DISC
C5—100 μF, 15 VOLT
D1, D2, D3—1N914

Q1, Q2, Q3, Q5—2N2222
Q4—FET, BS-170
IC1—555 TIMER
S1—DPDT SWITCH
S2—DPDT SWITCH
J1, J2, J3, J4—INPUT AND OUTPUT JACKS
BANANA JACKS

49

until the attack phase has been completed (Q2 is bypassed when S1 is in the manual mode).

When IC1 is triggered, its output (at pin 3), goes high and charges C3 through D2, R6, and R7. Attack time is set by potentiometer R7 and ranges from a few milliseconds to almost 10 seconds. Diode D1 and D2 ensure that no interaction between attack and decay function is possible, while transistor Q4 denies any other discharge path to capacitor C3. When the attack and sustain portions of the envelope have been completed, IC1 turns off and its output goes low, creating a discharge path for capacitor C3 through resistor R8, R9, and diode D3.

What makes this design special is the unique attribute of voltage-controlled decay. Switch S2 enables the selection of linear or exponential decay; closer examination shows how this is achieved. In the diagram, switch S3 is in the linear position, but when switched to the exponential position, the output is fed back to transistor Q3 through resistor R14 and R10. When the output goes high, Q3 turns on and enables capacitor C3 to discharge through resistor R8 and diode D3. As C3 discharges, the output of the module changes and therefore gradually shuts off Q3. This feedback network produces a gently sloping curve at the output. By taking the output through an attenuator and then to jack J3 while switch S2 is in the linear position, virtually any output curve can be attained. The foil pattern for the envelope generator is shown in Fig. 5-3.

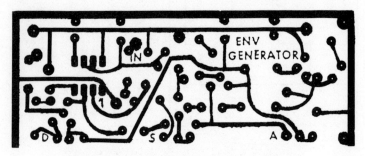

Fig. 5-3. Foil pattern for envelope generator.

The importance of the voltage-controlled input cannot be stressed enough because it is the key to precise and ultimate control. The possibilities for this design are quite literally infinite. Some of the most interesting and ambitious applications follow.

The first benefit derived from this circuit is exponential envelopes including a reverse exponential envelope (which must be heard to be believed). Figure 5-4 shows the output of the generator when switch S2 is in the exponential position. Figure 5-5 shows the output when fed back to the control voltage input through an inverter and is one of the most interesting envelopes to hear.

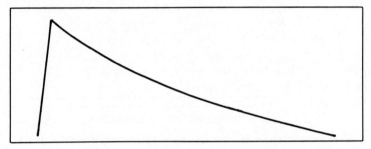

Fig. 5-4. Exponential decay waveshape.

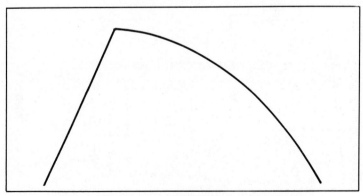

Fig. 5-5. Reverse exponential decay waveshape.

It is in the linear position that the module becomes its most versatile because it puts total control of the envelope into the hands of the user. Envelopes like the one in Fig. 5-6 are easily obtainable with the use of a simple attenuator. Imagine what a clarinet would sound like with the envelope of a snare drum or what a complex digital source (from a digital synthesizer) would sound like with a reverse exponential envelope. These new envelopes can expand the musical vocabulary of even the most sophisticated and ambitious composer, and we've only begun to explore the possibilities.

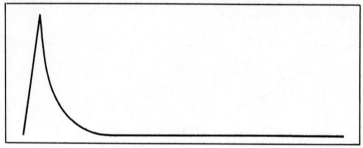

Fig. 5-6. Percussion decay waveshape.

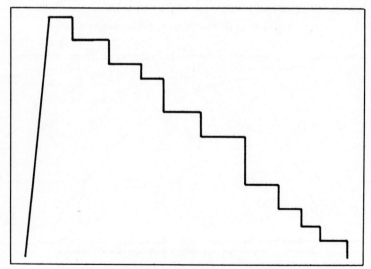

Fig. 5-7. Ten-stage, step-decay waveshape.

Digital synthesizers are capable of producing multistage envelopes with six or seven stages. If you need more, use the module of Fig. 5-2. The maximum time of the envelope (attack, sustain, and decay) is approximately 30 seconds, which should be plenty of time for as many stages as you are likely to need.

When used with the sequencer (that appears in Chapter 6), 10, 20, or even 30 or more envelope stages can be achieved as Fig. 5-7 illustrates. Both linear and exponential elements can be programmed within a single envelope in any proportion or arrangement. Figure 5-8 shows one of these complex envelopes and Fig. 5-9 depicts a linear, exponential, reverse exponential envelope.

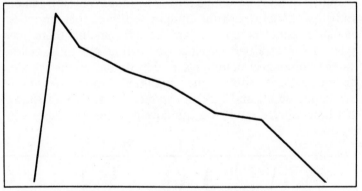

Fig. 5-8. Multistage linear and exponential decay waveshape.

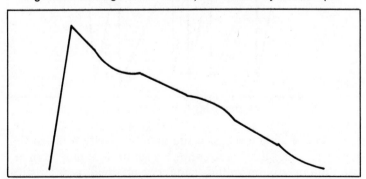

Fig. 5-9. Multistage linear, exponential, and reverse exponential decay waveshape.

The feature that might be the most important of all is the capability to change instantaneously. The envelopes of instruments, other than electronic, are basically controlled by the player. Electronic envelope generators are preset and do not allow the player to make quick changes. Sequencers without envelope changes can sound too mechanical and keyboards without envelope changes can sound bland and lacking in character.

The control voltage for the module of Fig. 5-2 can originate from a multitude of sources such as a foot pedal when using a keyboard, a sequencer row to generate a more interesting and varied pattern, or a click track that is synchronized with other tracks. Figure 5-10 shows a diagram of the changing of the decay slope during a random envelope chain and thus demonstrates the unique ability of this circuit to change parameters in an instant. This means that there now exists a sophisticated envelope-generating system to match the incredible new techniques used by digital synthesizers in the production of source tones. In Fig. 5-11, a mixture of linear, exponential, and reverse exponential envelopes shows just how much control you can have over the envelopes you produce.

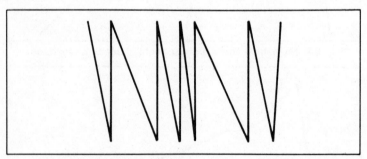

Fig. 5-10. Quick-changing, linear-decay envelope chain.

Note: If switch S1 is in the manual position (as in the schematic) and the attack control is set for too long an interval, then maximum volume cannot be attained. Similar situations can arise involving the sustain and decay—remember

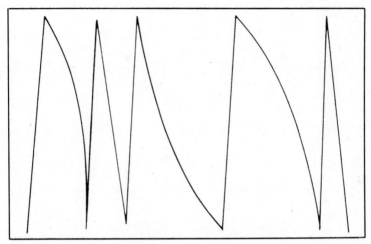

Fig. 5-11. Quick-changing, linear-decay, and exponential-decay envelope chain.

that these controls can override the effects of control voltages, so take care when adjusting them.

Envelope generation is obviously the main function of an envelope generator, but there are other duties that are ideally suited to this unit. Filter control is the most common secondary use, but one of the most interesting potentials is its ability to generate extremely complex waveforms. An envelope generator is usually thought of as a low-frequency controller of VCAs and VCFs, but this device can operate at high frequency and can serve as a frequency and amplitude modulating source for VCOs and VCAs. Combined with a sequencer and an electronic switch, it is possible to produce complex waveforms with methods not unlike those used by digital synthesizers. The number of stages, speed of sequence, and type of modulation used are all factors that determine the resultant waveform.

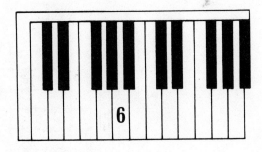

Sequencers

ALL OF THE CIRCUITS IN THIS CHAPTER ARE extremely versatile and can be used in an enormous variety of musical or sound-processing situations.

A *sequencer* is a device for producing a series of preset control voltages to provide rhythms, arpeggios, and frequency modulation. There are many types and designs, but because of its remarkable versatility, this chapter includes one comprehensive 10-stage circuit.

The 4017 was chosen for its ability to provide full power-supply voltage without the need for output buffers. Referring to Fig. 6-1, switch S1 enables the user to select any number of stages from 1 to 10. A pulse injected at J2 while S1 is set at position 10 resets the count to 1 and thus permits an external source to continually change the number of stages. Ten LEDs indicate which stage is in use, and there is a pulse output for each stage. A total of 30 linear taper potentiometers act as adjustable voltage dividers and output three different control voltages. Diodes isolate the output and prevent interaction between controls while the 1 megohm resistors apply ground reference and the 1 kilohm resistors limit the current at the output. Switch S2 selects either an internal clock generator (as described in Chapter 2) or an external clock. Figure 6-2

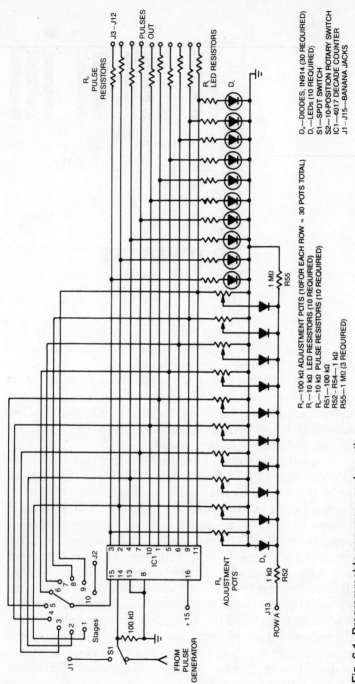

Fig. 6-1. Programmable sequencer schematic.

R_w PULSE RESISTORS

J3 – J12

PULSES OUT

R_r LED RESISTORS

D_L

D_d—DIODES, IN914 (30 REQUIRED)
D_L—LEDs (10 REQUIRED)
S1—SPDT SWITCH
S2—10-POSITION ROTARY SWITCH
IC1—4017 DECADE COUNTER
J1 – J15—BANANA JACKS

1 MΩ R55

R_a—100 kΩ ADJUSTMENT POTS (10 FOR EACH ROW = 30 POTS TOTAL)
R_r—10 kΩ LED RESISTORS (10 REQUIRED)
R_p—10 kΩ PULSE RESISTORS (10 REQUIRED)
R51—100 kΩ
R52 - R54— 1 kΩ
R55—1 MΩ (3 REQUIRED)

IC1

R_a ADJUSTMENT POTS

D_A

J13 ○ ROW A
1 kΩ R52

100 kΩ

FROM PULSE GENERATOR

+15

S1

J1 ○

J2

Stages

ADJUSTMENT POTS

58

shows how three different parameters—pitch, tone, and amplitude—can be controlled simultaneously. The foil pattern for the sequencer is in Fig. 6-3.

This remarkable circuit can, when combined with the envelope generator in Chapter 5, produce some of the most unusual envelopes and frequency-modulating control voltages. The sequencer can be triggered by the MIDI interface (Chapter 11) to provide rhythm accompaniment or tamboral generation for sampling and storage.

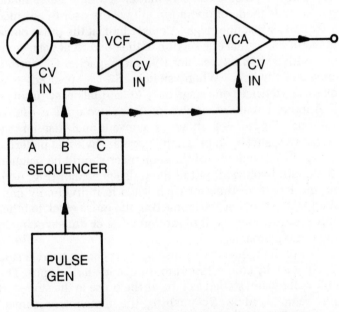

Fig. 6-2. Multiparameter sequencer control block diagram.

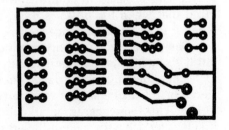

Fig. 6-3. Foil pattern for programmable sequencer.

The pulse outputs can be used to stop the clock generator for short sequences, or you can use all of them to trigger 10 different events. They can also be used to produce accents, trigger other sequencers, create click tracks, trigger multiple envelopes, or divide MIDI pulse trains.

The sequencer used together with the pulse generator (described in Chapter 2) form a unique control facility. Switch S3, on the pulse clock, provides access to the pulse output when it is in the up position, but in the down position (as in the pulse clock schematic), a single pulse mode engages. This mode of operation allows the user to advance the sequencer just one stage. A closer look at the pulse clock schematic shows that one section of the quad NOR gate, combined with switch S2, resistor R5, and capacitor C7, form a bounceless switch. When switch S2 is pressed, the sequencer advances one stage only to facilitate easy tuning.

Another benefit of combining these two units is timing variations. Figure 6-4 shows a conventional regular sequencer waveshape. To program irregular rhythmic patterns, an output from one row of the sequencer should be patched to the control voltage input of the pulse generator (Fig. 6-5). Now the length of time for each stage is individually controlled by the sequencer. Connecting the pulse clock to other control sources can result in randomizing or time-syncing to some other parameter.

Any of the sequencer's pulse outputs can be used to stop the sequence by connecting it to the "stop-start" input. The count will remain stalled as long as the pulse to the stop-start input remains high. By pushing the momentary contact switch S2, you can manually start the sequence. Any pulse source can be used to control the sequencer. Just keep in mind that when the pulse is high, the sequence stops and when it is low, the sequence continues.

The pulse clock not only produces a pulse at its output but it also generates an alternate output. Output jacks J2 and J3 access the pulses to trigger such effects as ping-pong stereo or other effects that require two out-of-phase trigger pulses. This sequencer is remarkably flexible, as it must be if it is to interface with state-of-the-art digital equipment.

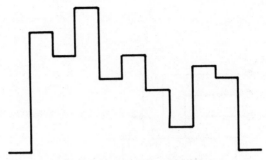

Fig. 6-4. Sequencer waveshape.

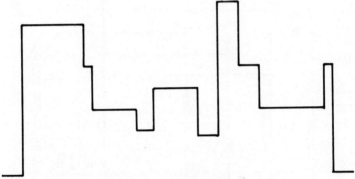

Fig. 6-5. Irregular rhythmic sequencer pattern.

ELECTRONIC SWITCH

In the schematic of the sequencer (Fig. 6-1), only one row of outputs is shown for the sake of clarity. There are actually three rows of output to supply three different and individually adjustable control voltages.

It might be necessary to generate a sequence of more than 10 events, facilitating the use of an electronic switch (Fig. 6-6). This circuit again uses the 4017, but this time it is restricted to two or three stages. The LEDs indicate which of the inputs passes to the output. A bilateral switch has the duty of transferring information, and because of the characteristics of the IC, it can carry signals in both directions. Outputs from rows A, B, and C of the sequencer can be

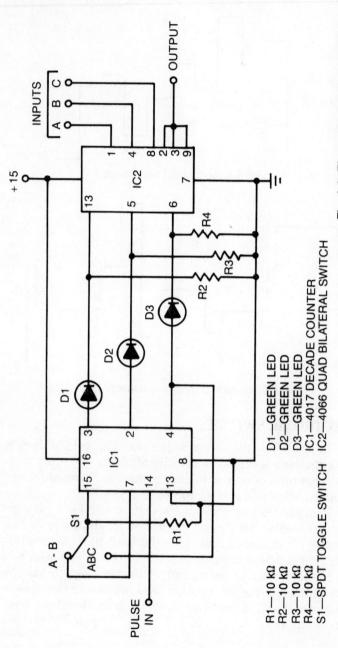

Fig. 6-6. Electronic switch schematic.

R1—10 kΩ
R2—10 kΩ
R3—10 kΩ
R4—10 kΩ
S1—SPDT TOGGLE SWITCH

D1—GREEN LED
D2—GREEN LED
D3—GREEN LED
IC1—4017 DECADE COUNTER
IC2—4066 QUAD BILATERAL SWITCH

connected to the three inputs of the electronic switch (see Fig. 6-7), and a pulse output is chosen from the sequencer and fed to the pulse input of the electronic switch. When the switch receives a pulse, it changes to the next row, expanding the sequencer to 30 stages. This circuit can pass any kind of signal—audio, control voltages, MIDI—and switch S1 facilitates the selection of either two or three inputs. Figure 6-8 shows the foil pattern for the electronic switch.

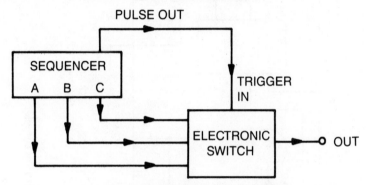

Fig. 6-7. Stage expansion block diagram.

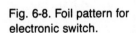 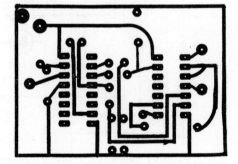

Fig. 6-8. Foil pattern for electronic switch.

SAMPLER

The average sequence is about four to eight notes long, but occasionally you might need 20 or 30 stages. Even more rare is the need for sequences beyond 30 stages, but it is always a good idea to include those modules in your system for which you might have only occasional need. One such

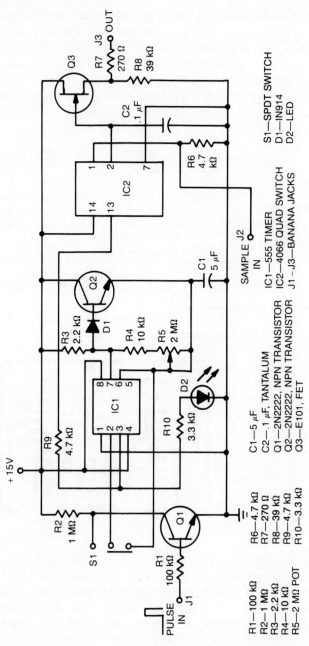

Fig. 6-9. Schematic of sampler.

S1—SPDT SWITCH
D1—IN914
D2—LED

IC1—555 TIMER
IC2—4066 QUAD SWITCH
J1 – J3—BANANA JACKS

C1—5 µF, TANTALUM
C2—.1 µF
Q1—2N2222, NPN TRANSISTOR
Q2—2N2222, NPN TRANSISTOR
Q3—E101, FET

R1—100 kΩ
R2—1 MΩ
R3—2.2 kΩ
R4—10 kΩ
R5—2 MΩ POT

R6—4.7 kΩ
R7—270 Ω
R8—39 kΩ
R9—4.7 kΩ
R10—3.3 kΩ

module is a *sampler*. It can produce sequences with literally hundreds of stages. The schematic, shown in Fig. 6-9 shows IC1 used as a needle pulse generator. This extremely short pulse is necessary to prevent the holding section from following the sampled wave.

Switch S1 changes IC1 from a pulse generator to a pulse processor that maintains its pulse width regardless of the input pulse width. Diode D2 serves as a visual monitor of the pulse while potentiometer R5 determines the frequency when S1 puts IC1 in the generator mode. Almost any waveshape can be sampled, however square waves and pulses should be avoided. Figure 6-10 is a diagram illustrating the way the sampler functions. When a pulse is sensed by IC2 through pin 13, it briefly passes the signal from pin 1 to pin 2 of IC2.

Resistor R6 discharges capacitor C2 and leaves a charge equal to the signal level at the time of the pulse. When the pulse is gone, capacitor C2 is denied any discharge path, so transistor Q3 is held at a fixed level until the next pulse.

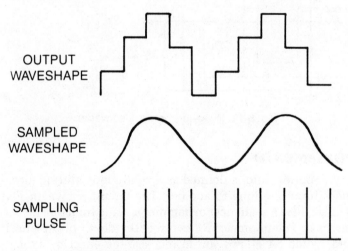

Fig. 6-10. Function diagram of sampler.

SINE WAVE CONVERTER

Figure 6-11 shows the schematic of a sine wave converter. A low-frequency sine wave can be generated from a continuous pulse train. This is achieved by the accumulated effects of multiple charging and discharging paths presented to capacitor C2 by four buffered gates. Grounding the so-called "jam" inputs (pins 2, 3, 7, 9, and 12) ensures that the output frequency is $1/10$ that of the input, which makes it a perfect sweep output for the 10-stage sequencer. The output can also provide an excellent source for the sampler and can sync the sampler with the 10-stage sequencer.

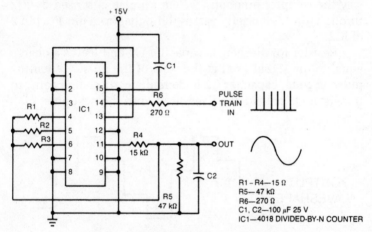

Fig. 6-11. Pulse-to-sine wave converter.

PORTAMENTO

A *portamento* is defined as a continuous gliding movement from one tone to another. The circuit shown in Fig. 6-12 enables a sequencer or sampler to slide from one note to the next. Potentiometer R3 controls the depth of the effect, and switch S1 allows you to increase the effect by a factor of 10.

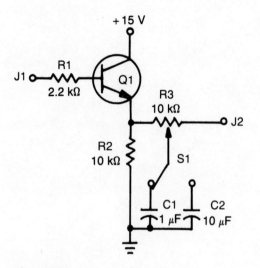

R1—2.2 kΩ
R2—10 kΩ
R3— 10 kΩ POT
C1—1 μF
C2—10 μF
S1—SPDT TOGGLE SWITCH
Q1—2N3565, NPN TRANSISTOR

Fig. 6-12. Portamento schematic.

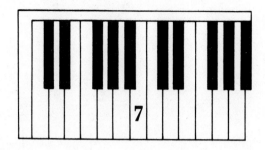

Keyboards

CHAPTERS UP TO THIS POINT HAVE DISCUSS-
ed several ways to control the frequency of pitch sources.
This chapter deals only with manual methods of achieving
this end. Manual control devices used in the past include
light-control devices, ribbon controllers, touch-plate keyboards, a magnetically sensitive device that registers minute
changes in the earth's magnetic field, and instruments called
theremins that used the body capacitance of the musician to
alter the frequency of the sound. The type of control you
choose depends on your experience, but keep in mind that
some controllers are easily mastered and can produce
impressive sounds.

RIBBON CONTROLLER

This project is very unusual in that it utilizes the electrical properties of some common household items. For example, resistor R2 of Fig. 7-1 is actually a piece of balsa wood
measuring $1/2$ inch by $1/8$ inch by 22 inches. It's covered with
a 50-percent india ink/50-percent saline solution (salt water).
This coated wood acts as a voltage divider when connected
across a power supply. Probe P1 picks off a voltage from R2

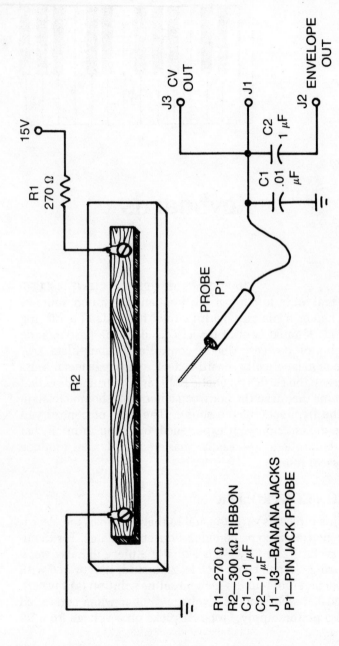

R1—270 Ω
R2—300 kΩ RIBBON
C1—.01 µF
C2—1 µF
J1–J3—BANANA JACKS
P1—PIN JACK PROBE

Fig. 7-1. Ribbon controller.

and outputs it to J1 and through C2, providing an envelope output. Capacitor C1 removes noise that is produced when the probe is moved along the ribbon. The ribbon should be glued to a strong support board and connected to the 15-volt supply through a 270-ohm resistor. The other end of the ribbon is connected to ground.

To prepare the ribbon, mix a tablespoon of india ink with an equal amount of salt water. Apply a generous coat with a small brush to all sides of the wood to ensure continuity and proper probe contact. Use a soldering lug, washer, and round-headed wood screw to mount the ribbon to the support (Fig. 7-2). Drill a small hole in the support board to run a wire to the power supply, and tape the end of the board to prevent direct contact between the screw assemblies and the probe.

After mounting the ribbon and connecting it to the power supply, test the unit with a voltmeter. You should get a reading of just under 15 volts on the right "high" side of the ribbon. As you slide the test probe to the left, the voltage should drop to just above 0 volts at the left end of the ribbon. If there is a breach in continuity or the ribbon is worn, it can be recoated with solution while still mounted.

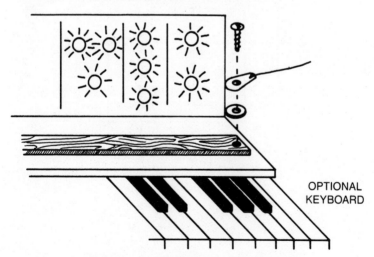

Fig. 7-2. Mounting details for ribbon controller.

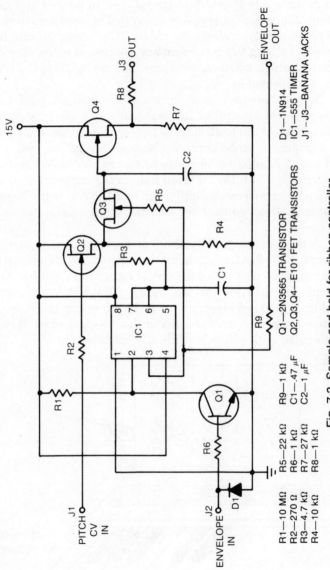

Fig. 7-3. Sample and hold for ribbon controller.

Q1—2N3565 TRANSISTOR
Q2,Q3,Q4—E101 FET TRANSISTORS
D1—1N914
IC1—555 TIMER
J1–J3—BANANA JACKS

R1—10 MΩ
R2—270 Ω
R3—4.7 kΩ
R4—10 kΩ
R5—22 kΩ
R6—1 kΩ
R7—27 kΩ
R8—1 kΩ
R9—1 kΩ
C1—47 μF
C2—1 μF

SAMPLE-AND-HOLD CIRCUIT

The ribbon controller needs some help in producing a usable signal, and the sample-and-hold circuit in Fig. 7-3 was designed for just that purpose. When the probe touches the ribbon, a voltage is selected and goes to transistor Q2 through resistor R2. At the same time, transistor Q1 receives a decoupled signal. The triggering of Q1 activates 555 timer IC1, which turns on transistor Q3 and puts out an envelope trigger. Transistor Q4 receives the voltage through Q2, which either charges capacitor C2 to a higher voltage or discharges it to a lower voltage through resistor R4. Capacitor C2 has no discharge path when Q3 turns off, so transistor Q4 stays partially on.

Playing the ribbon is very simple. Touch the probe to the ribbon and you should hear a pitch rise and fall relative to the setting of the envelope generator (Fig. 7-4). As the probe moves up or down, the pitch will slide to a new pitch and then decay. If there is a need to produce a pitch that remains as long as the probe is on the ribbon, take the envelop from J3 of the probe rather than J2. The foil pattern is shown in Fig. 7-5.

The highest pitch should be produced only when the probe is almost at the end of the right side of the ribbon and should start descending with just an inch or two to the left. If this does not happen, replace resistor R2 of the sample and hold circuit with a resistor of higher value. Many unusual effects can be generated with this controller, and with a little practice, you can create your own new and interesting techniques.

STEPPED KEYBOARD

A more conventional approach to manual controllers is the *stepped keyboard*, which is the most common control device. Figure 7-6 illustrates a series voltage divider that, while effective, is difficult to tune because changing any one trim potentiometer changes the entire divider. A solution to this problem is shown in Fig. 7-7 where each step is its own voltage divider and has no effect on any other step.

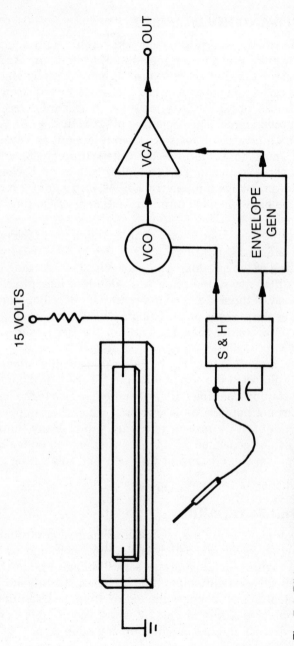

Fig. 7-4. Ribbon controller block diagram.

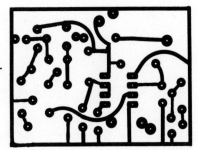

Fig. 7-5. Foil pattern for sample-
and-hold ribbon controller.

There are many problems associated with building your own mechanical keyboard, not the least of which is expense. Precision is absolutely necessary, as well as uniformity and durability, which makes putting your own keyboard together quite a formidable task. Consider also that surplus electronic supply houses often sell keyboards at very reasonable prices. The keyboard used with the small system in Chapter 10 was purchased for under $100. All switch contacts on these keyboards are gold plated to assure noise-free contact.

LINEAR-TO-EXPONENTIAL KEYBOARD

If you experiment a lot with keyboard circuits, you will discover that a linear voltage divider will not produce a diatonic scale. To take advantage of the stability of a linear voltage divider and still produce an exponential output, use a *linear-to-exponential converter*. In Fig. 7-8, a linear voltage divider feeds a linear integrated circuit. Transistor Q1 is in the feedback loop of IC1 and therefore imparts its exponential response to the integrated circuit. All fixed resistors in the voltage divider should be 100-ohm, 1-percent precision resistors. Potentiometers R7 and R8 will match the divider to the number of octaves of the keyboard, while R4 and R6 adjust the exponential curve to match the range of the voltage divider. Tuning is a matter of achieving a balance between the two sets of potentiometers, which can be somewhat tricky, so make sure that R7 and R8 are adjusted first to establish proper range.

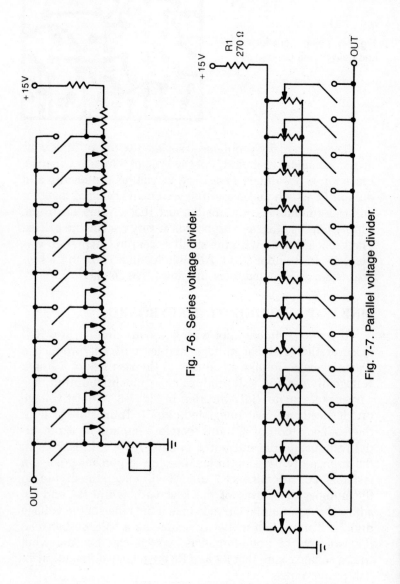

Fig. 7-6. Series voltage divider.

Fig. 7-7. Parallel voltage divider.

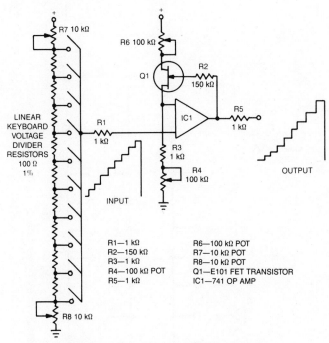

Fig. 7-8. Linear to exponential keyboard.

STRING KEYBOARD

The *string keyboard* is named not for the sound it makes but for the fact that it utilizes an india-ink-coated piece of string for its voltage divider. Use an absorbent type of string such as wrapping twine. Mount the string with screweyes as shown in Fig. 7-9 with a spring at one end to maintain tension.

Attach wires to the string by twisting the wire once around the string and then slide it to the left or right to tune. The wiring diagram for the string keyboard is shown in Fig. 7-10.

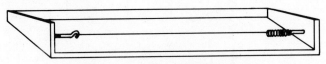

Fig. 7-9. String keyboard diagram.

77

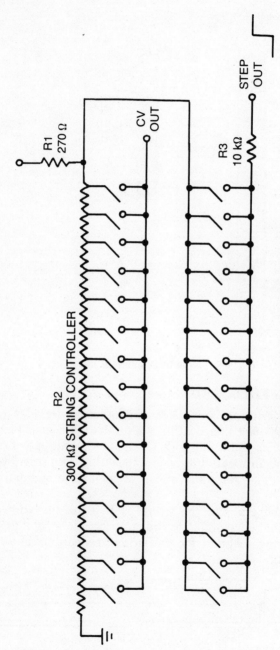

Fig. 7-10. Mounting details for string keyboard.

TOUCH PLATE KEYBOARD

Another type of keyboard is the touch plate keyboard which switches from one note to another electronically. Figure 7-11 shows a touch plate circuit that uses a series of electronic latches to hold position. If key one is pressed, transistor Q8 turns on, which applies negative bias to transistor Q1 and turns it on. Resistor R8 enables transistor Q1 to forward bias Q8 and therefore the two transistors keep each other in a fixed or latched state.

When a new key is pressed, transistor Q16 turns on and through the two timer ICs, turns off transistor Q15 for a split second. This action unlatches the key that is in service and latches the new key into service.

The pitch is tuned through the potentiometer that is connected to the latch that is in service. The diodes keep the latch from interacting. Resistor R22 is a current limiter. An envelope signal is furnished by timer IC1, which remains on as long as a key is pressed.

Only seven stages are shown due to a lack of space, but any number of stages can be added. Another row of output potentiometers can also be added to provide another row of control voltage outputs. Touch plate keyboards generally have fewer keys than conventional keyboards, but this is not a handicap because all of the keys can be tuned to the composition so that all keys are used. A second row of controls can facilitate quick key changes and a row of LEDs can be added to indicate the key in service.

An actual-size foil pattern guide is shown in Fig. 7-12. The circuit board can be etched with as many keys as the board will allow. The row of holes across the top of the circuit board provide connecting points for all of the individual key inputs, while at the lower left corner of the circuit board is a single hole that is to be connected to the circuit at the point marked "touch plate in."

When soldering wires to the board, keep in mind that hands come in contact with the foil, so clip the excess wire close and lightly sand the solder points smooth with a nail board or light sandpaper. The keyboard should be mounted

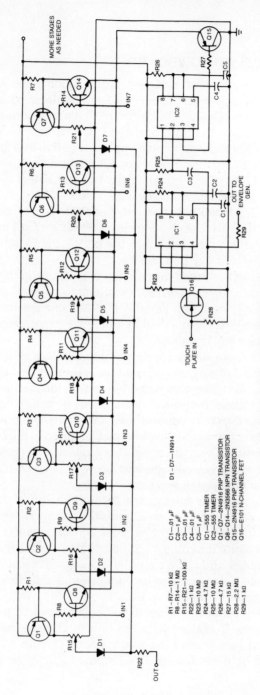

Fig. 7-11. Schematic of touch plate keyboard.

Fig. 7-12. Keyboard foil pattern.

to a firmly supported section of the faceplate and then coated with a thin layer of varnish. The copper will remain clean and shiny, and the varnish will in no way interfere with the normal operation of the keyboard.

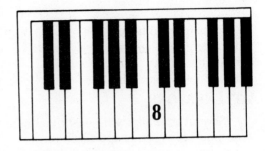

Attenuators
and
Processors

CONTROL VOLTAGES OFTEN NEED FINE TUN-
ing to achieve a given effect, and there may be no capability
for this included in the module. The circuits in this chapter
are designed to meet a variety of control and interface situations.

Attenuators can be applied to external signals that
exceed the power supply of the synthesizer, but make sure
that the control is set to the minimum position and advance
the control slowly until you attain the desired effect. Then
connect the signal to another attenuator for range adjustment; only this control should be adjusted. Disconnect this
type of interface as soon as possible to avoid accidents or
damage. High-voltage interface can be very tricky, so it is not
recommended to the uninitiated.

If a control voltage is of the wrong polarity, it can be connected to the inverter described in Chapter 9 and then dis-
tributed to any of the attenuators. The inverter circuit can
increase the amplitude of its input, so make adjustments
accordingly.

The circuits in this chapter might seem very simple, but
they are indispensable when it comes to the precise control

of synthesizer voltage parameters. All of the attenuators in this chapter are passive devices and can only reduce signal amplitude.

ATTENUATORS

Several attenuators are described here that produce various effects for various applications.

DUAL ATTENUATOR

A dual potentiometer (see Fig. 8-1) can synchronize manual changes made in two separate control voltages for two separate modules. A control voltage fed to jack J1 and an inverted version of the same voltage fed to J2 can produce interesting pitch-crossing effects, manual or manual override panning, and manual override filter sweep warbles. Figures 8-2 through 8-5 illustrate the versatility of this simple but useful circuit.

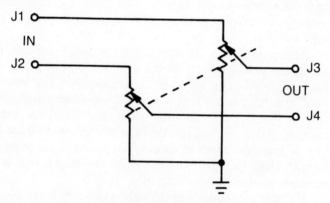

R1—100 kΩ Dual Pot
J1 – J4—Banana Jacks

Fig. 8-1. Dual attenuator.

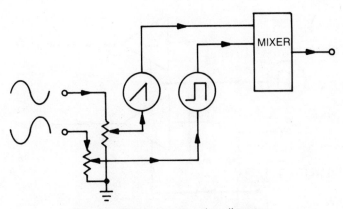

Fig. 8-2. Frequency-crossing diagram.

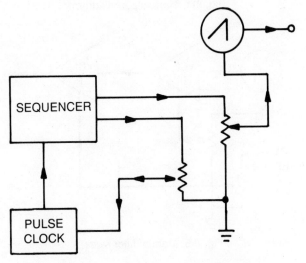

Fig. 8-3. Speed- and pitch-coordinating diagram.

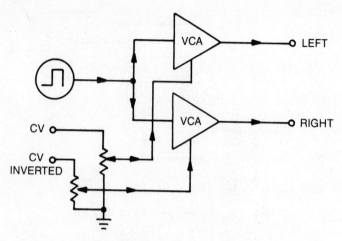

Fig. 8-4. Manual pan diagram.

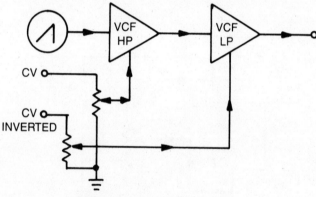

Fig. 8-5. Manual filter sweep.

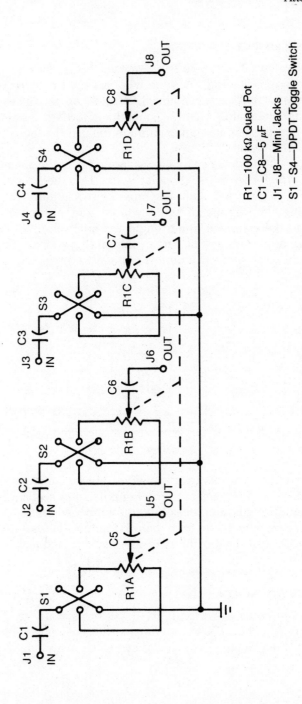

Fig. 8-6. Synchronous attenuator.

R1—100 kΩ Quad Pot
C1 – C8—5 μF
J1 – J8—Mini Jacks
S1 – S4—DPDT Toggle Switch

SYNCHRONOUS ATTENUATOR

It is often necessary to fade two or more signals at the same time (crossfading). Anyone who has tried to synchronize this activity knows just how difficult it can be. The synchronous attenuator enables smooth, effortless manual control of four separate signals through the use of a four-section potentiometer.

Figure 8-6 shows a switch for each section of the potentiometer, which can reverse its polarity to set up the circuit to crossfade. Figure 8-7 shows a crossfade diagram, where increasing the volume of the sawtooth and pulse waves decreases the volume of the triangle and sine waves. Crossfades are a very important part of the mixing process, and this module can perform a perfect crossfade every time.

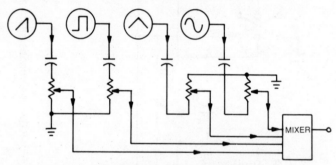

Fig. 8-7. Crossfade diagram.

Any of the controls in this chapter can be combined in any fashion or arrangement. For example, two sequencers combined through the processor can then be fed to the control voltage expander and from there to four oscillators whose outputs are connected to the sync attenuator, which is set for crossfade.

OPEN ATTENUATOR

As simple as this circuit is, it performs many useful functions (Fig. 8-8). The circuit only consists of a potentiometer and three banana jacks, but it can solve many interface problems. Figure 8-9 shows an adjustable ring modulator. Figures 8-10 and 8-11 show a control voltage cross-fader and a low-frequency oscillator balancing patch, respectively.

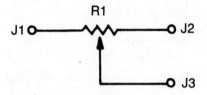

R1—1 MΩ POT
J1 – J3—BANANA JACKS

Fig. 8-8. Open attenuator.

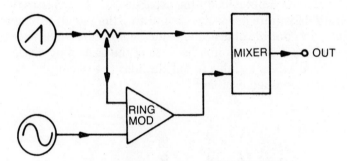

Fig. 8-9. Adjustable ring modulator diagram.

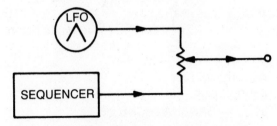

Fig. 8-10. Open attenuator crossfader diagram.

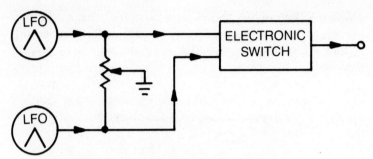

Fig. 8-11. Open attenuator balancing diagram.

DECOUPLING ATTENUATOR

Decoupling control voltages can produce some very interesting effects. Referring to Fig. 8-12 capacitor C1 decouples the input while C2 decouples the output. Jack J2 bypasses the input decoupling capacitor and J3 bypasses the output decoupling capacitor, converting the circuit to a conventional control voltage attenuator. Sequencers are an excellent source for decoupling because of the cascading pitches produced when a pulse is fed through the decoupler to a voltage-controlled oscillator.

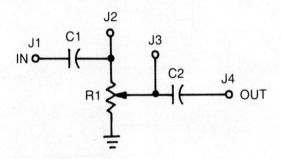

R1—100 kΩ POT
C1,C2—5 μF
J1 – J4—BANANA JACKS

Fig. 8-12. Decoupling attenuator.

FEEDBACK ATTENUATION

Many synthesizer modules can have their normal output altered through the use of feedback. One example of this is a change in pulse width of a square wave, when an oscillator's output is fed back to its frequency modulated input. Attenuators can provide precise control of feedback loops and can even offer alternatives such as multiphase dual-loop interlock.

Sequencers can also benefit from such techniques as multipath feedback and link coordination. The latter involves the extraction of a MIDI pulse train and converting it to a synchronized modulating frequency.

OTHER CONTROL CIRCUITS

The following circuits can be used with the various attenuators to provide you with even more versatility and control.

PROCESSOR

The processor is an indispensible circuit for parameter trimming and interface adjustment (Fig. 8-13). A sequencer

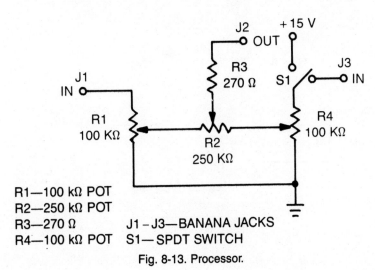

R1—100 kΩ POT
R2—250 kΩ POT
R3—270 Ω
R4—100 kΩ POT

J1–J3—BANANA JACKS
S1—SPDT SWITCH

Fig. 8-13. Processor.

can be diverted from its normal tuning with a gliding action provided by an LFO (Fig. 8-14), or use a second sequencer to determine the key of the first (Fig. 8-15). Try a range-adjusting configuration as in Fig. 8-16.

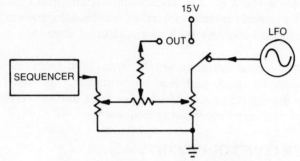

Fig. 8-14. Sequencer gliding diagram.

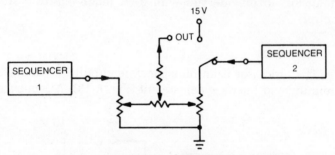

Fig. 8-15. Two-sequencer interface diagram.

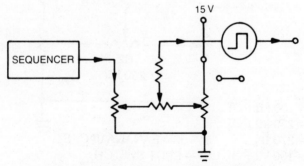

Fig. 8-16. Sequencer range-adjustment diagram.

CONTROL VOLTAGE EXPANDER

This circuit can be used with any module, but it is most useful in feeding a single control voltage to an oscillator bank (Fig. 8-17). Figure 8-18 shows a sequencer feeding four separate oscillators. The intervals of each oscillator can be individually tuned to produce chords from a single control voltage.

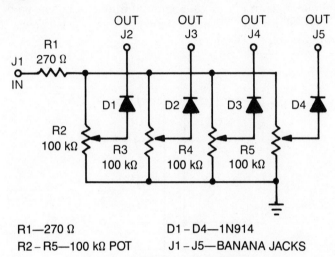

R1—270 Ω   D1 – D4—1N914
R2 – R5—100 kΩ POT   J1 – J5—BANANA JACKS

Fig. 8-17. Control-voltage expander.

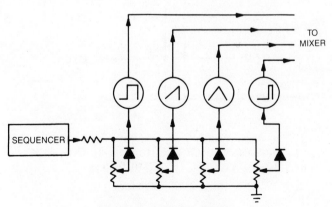

Fig. 8-18. Expander diagram.

PATCH BAY

The patch bay facilitates interfacing to other synthesizers or processing equipment (Fig. 8-19). Jacks J1 through J4 are mini jacks, while all remaining jacks are an assortment of standard connectors. Six of the jacks have decoupling capacitors, making this module suitable for audio as well as control-voltage interface. When combined with the decoupling attenuator, as in Fig. 8-20, a manual filter can be engaged. If you need an impedance reference, Fig. 8-21 shows the proper patch arrangement.

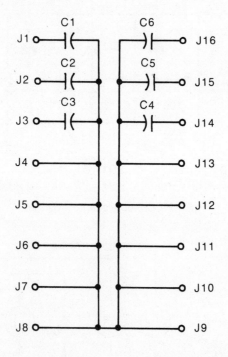

J1 – J4—MINI JACKS   J11 – J12—PIN JACKS
J5 – J8—BANANA JACKS   J13 – J16—PHONE JACKS
J9 – J10—RCA JACKS   C1 – C6—5 μF

Fig. 8-19. Patch bay.

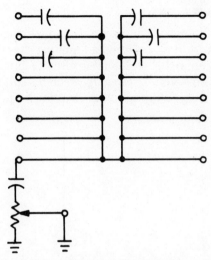

Fig. 8-20. Manual filter, using patch bay and decoupling attenuator.

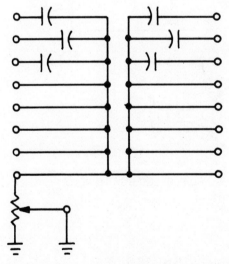

Fig. 8-21. Patch bay with adjustable ground reference.

GLITCH-FREE CONTROL

All potentiometers can become clogged or gritty, which can result in distorted sound when moving the control. This can be merely annoying with analog circuits, but with digital circuits it could mean disaster. A practical solution to this problem is displayed in Fig. 8-22. Resistor R1 provides pro-

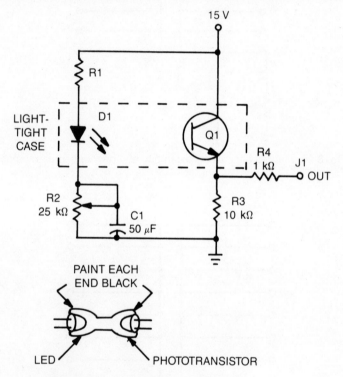

R1—SELECTED FOR LED BRIGHTNESS

R2—25 kΩ POT

R3—10 kΩ

R4—1 kΩ

D1—LED

Q1—LIGHT-SENSITIVE TRANSISTOR

C1—50 μF

J1—BANANA JACK

Fig. 8-22. No glitch control.

tection and must also drive D1 to full brightness. Since this varies from one diode to the next, select R1 by experimentation. Construct the light-tight case from a piece of heatshrink tubing, and be sure to put a touch of black paint on the ends of the device to prevent light from entering through the LED or phototransistor. Capacitor C1 acts as a filter to smooth out any spikes that might be induced by potentiometer R2.

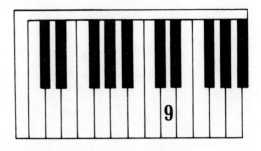

Miscellaneous Circuits

THIS CHAPTER IS DEVOTED TO CIRCUITS that are very useful but for one reason or another defy categorization. They all involve some unique form of signal processing that can enhance the performance of circuits described in this publication as well as analog or digital equipment you might already have.

INVERTER

The inverter circuit in Fig. 9-1 produces a voltage swing opposite of the input. Because of the circuit configuration and the use of a pnp transistor, a rise in input voltage produces a fall in output voltage. An additional feature of this unit is adjustable gain to accommodate a wide variety of signal levels. The circuit is very useful when you need to reverse an effect. You can also use it to feed the inverted voltage to a voltage-controlled amplifier or feed a noninverted voltage to another for signal panning.

OCTAVIZER

This circuit takes a signal and produces outputs of one, two, and three octaves below the input. Most of the work is

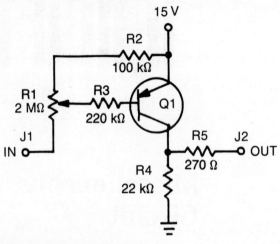

R1—2 MΩ LINEAR POT
R2—100 kΩ
R3—220 kΩ
R4—22 kΩ
R5—270 Ω
Q1—2N4916 PNP TRANSISTOR
J1 - J2—BANANA JACKS

Fig. 9-1. Inverter with gain.

performed by IC1 (see Fig. 9-2). Outputs are taken from J2, J3, and J4, but a more convenient composite signal is available at J5. Potentiometers R2, R3, R4, and R6 control the amount of mix, including the original tone. The sounds that emanate from this module are truly unusual.

FLANGER

Flanging is one of the most popular effects used in digital processors, and although this flanger is not as fancy as some digital versions, it is programmable.

Almost all linear ICs have a differential input, and much of their circuitry is designed to balance and compensate for these differences. When the 741 operational amplifier is biased at its positive input to a point equal to one-half of the

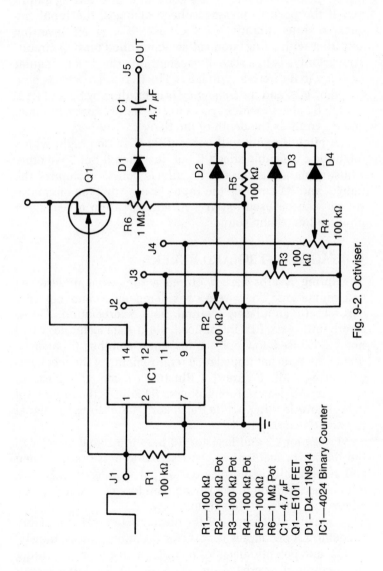

Fig. 9-2. Octiviser.

R1—100 kΩ
R2—100 kΩ Pot
R3—100 kΩ Pot
R4—100 kΩ Pot
R5—100 kΩ
R6—1 MΩ Pot
C1—4.7 µF
Q1—E101 FET
D1 – D4—1N914
IC1—4024 Binary Counter

power supply voltage and the input is fed to the negative input, the device operates as a conventional inverting amplifier. If the positive biasing voltage changes, the input frequency shifts slightly. In Fig. 9-3, IC1 is an inverting amplifier with a precision voltage-controlled biasing circuit. Transistor Q1 is in a state of constant flux due to a triangular wave fed to it through switch S1. The triangular wave is generated by IC2, and the frequency is controlled by S2 and R13. Switch S1 also provides access to an external control source, and R2 controls the depth of the flange.

A pitch dropout will occur if R2 is set too high, which might be a desirable effect; if not, just tune it out. Two other adjustments are included: R5 allows you to customize the flange, and R1 controls the input level. Any type of control voltage can be used—even step voltages from a sequencer produce interesting sounds.

VOLTAGE-CONTROLLED REVERB

Spring reverbs have acquired a somewhat undeserved bad reputation. They were considered noisy and not very accurate in simulating natural hall reverberation. When reverb units were first introduced, solid-state technology had not yet devised low-noise transistors. Another problem is due to the unusual impedance requirements of the mechanical spring unit. Figure 9-4 illustrates some new ideas in spring reverb design. Potentiometer R1 adjusts the input level to avoid overloading, while transistor Q1 amplifies the signal to drive the spring unit.

Capacitor C2 and Resistor R3 pass the signal directly to the output to maintain a good signal-to-noise ratio. When you remove all of the original signal and leave only that which passes through the spring, you lose clarity, and that's where this design differs from others.

Transistor Q2 amplifies the output of the spring unit and capacitor C3 decouples it. Resistor R4 reverse biases transistor Q2, and potentiometer R6 provides a means of controlling the amount of reverberation. Transistor Q3 performs a very

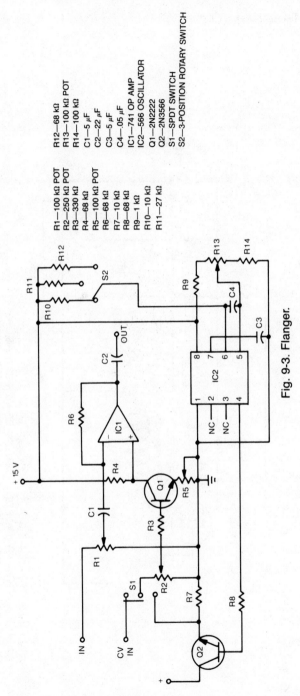

R1—100 kΩ POT
R2—250 kΩ POT
R3—330 kΩ
R4—68 kΩ
R5—100 kΩ POT
R6—68 kΩ
R7—10 kΩ
R8—68 kΩ
R9—1 kΩ
R10—10 kΩ
R11—27 kΩ

R12—68 kΩ
R13—100 kΩ POT
R14—100 kΩ
C1—5 μF
C2—22 μF
C3—5 μF
C4—.05 μF
IC1—741 OP AMP
IC2—566 OSCILLATOR
Q1—2N2222
Q2—2N3566
S1—SPDT SWITCH
S2—3-POSITION ROTARY SWITCH

Fig. 9-3. Flanger.

103

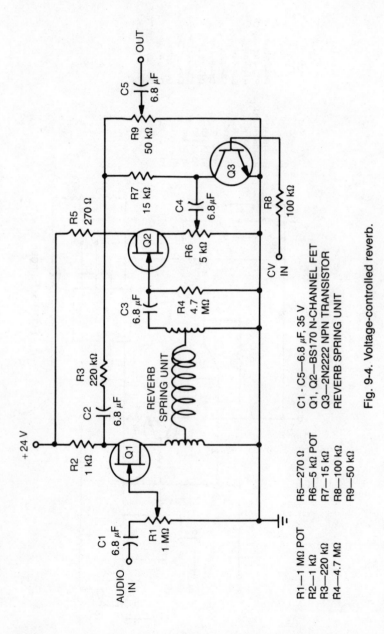

Fig. 9-4. Voltage-controlled reverb.

C1 - C5—6.8 µF, 35 V
Q1, Q2—BS170 N-CHANNEL FET
Q3—2N2222 NPN TRANSISTOR
REVERB SPRING UNIT

R1—1 MΩ POT
R2—1 kΩ
R3—220 kΩ
R4—4.7 MΩ

R5—270 Ω
R6—5 kΩ POT
R7—15 kΩ
R8—100 kΩ
R9—50 kΩ

unusual and useful task. It enables a control voltage to determine the amount of reverberation. This facilitates an enormous variety of high-speed precision effects that cannot be attained by any digital unit.

The reverb can be programmed to apply a different amount of reverberation to each note of a sequence. Even pulse signals can be used without producing "pops" in the audio. Envelope signals can also be used to control the reverb to produce unusual linear and exponential combinations.

High-speed operation can generate new tambors and enables this module to perform tasks that have never been thought possible. These new concepts require a rethinking of just what potential this module possesses.

AUTO PAN

Many interesting effects result from panning the audio from one channel to another. The schematic diagram for an auto pan is in Fig. 9-5. Transistors Q3 and Q4 ground the signal at the output through potentiometer R17. Both transistors are connected to the same source through resistors R13 and R14, but because they are of opposite polarity (npn and pnp), they alternate in their treatment of the signal. Potentiometer R17 sets the depth of the panning, and transistor Q2 isolates as well as amplifies the input signal.

A low-level triangular wave is generated by IC1 and is amplified to a usable level by transistor Q1. Rotary switch S2 and potentiometer R6 control the frequency of the panning, or switch S1 can select an external signal for this purpose.

This circuit can produce a wide range of panning effects—from slow undulating movement to high-speed stereo imaging. Much can be learned when experimenting with this module.

ENVELOPE DETECTOR

It occasionally becomes necessary to extract an envelope from an externally generated source. This can be accomplished with a circuit known as an *envelope detector*. Figure

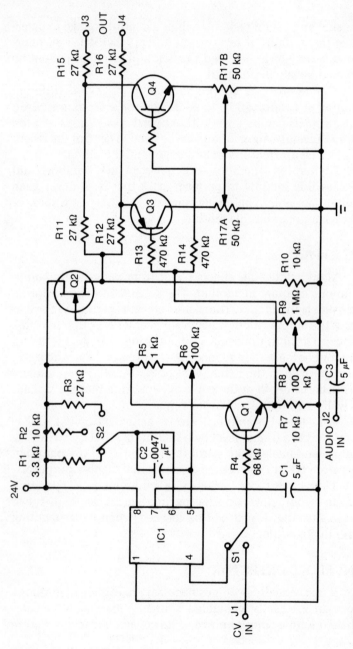

Fig. 9-5. Auto pan.

Parts List for Fig. 9-5.

R1—3.3 kΩ	R15—27 kΩ
R2—10 kΩ	R16—27 kΩ
R3—27 kΩ	R17A/B—50 kΩ DUAL POT
R4—68 kΩ	C1, C3—5μF
R5—1 kΩ	C2—.0047μF
R6—100 kΩ POT	Q1—2N3566, NPN
R7—10 kΩ	Q2—E101, FET
R8—100 kΩ	Q3—2N4916, PNP
R9—1 MΩ	Q4—2N3565, NPN
R10—10 kΩ	IC1—566, VCO
R11—27 KΩ	S1—SPDT
R12—27 kΩ	S2—3-Position Rotary
R13—470 kΩ	J1—Banana Jack
R14—470 kΩ	J2 – J4—Mini Jacks

9-6 illustrates what appears to be a preamp, but with one important difference—capacitor C2. Transistor Q1 receives an audio signal through capacitor C1 and potentiometer R1 and does function somewhat like a preamp, however as capacitor C2 is tuned closer to transistor Q2, there is a lag in response time as the second stage becomes more sensitive to the average level than to the actual frequency. When used with a white noise generator through a low-pass filter, this module serves as an excellent source for a sampler.

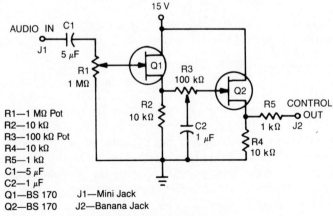

Fig. 9-6. Envelope detector.

RING MODULATOR

A ring modulator is a device that takes two audio inputs and produces an output equal to the sum and the difference between the signals. For example, an input of 900 Hz and a carrier of 300 Hz produce an output of 1200 Hz and 600 Hz. This might be of some mathematical interest, but it tells nothing about the character of the sound. A ring modulator is actually an amplitude modulator that enables a carrier frequency to control the amplitude of the input frequency.

An audio signal feeds to an interstage transformer (Fig. 9-7). The secondary of the transformer is connected to the

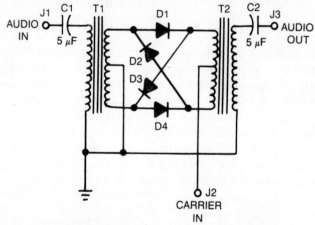

T1,T2—INTERSTAGE MINIATURE TRANSFORMER (SEE TEXT)
D1 – D4—1N914 DIODE
C1, C2—5 µF
J1 – J3—MINI JACKS

Fig. 9-7. Ring modulator.

secondary of an identical transformer through four diodes that form a control ring. The carrier frequency is introduced through the center taps of both transformers' secondaries. Diodes D1 through D4 are controlled by the carrier frequency so they consequently gate the input signal. A wide variety of transformers will work in this circuit, but they must be identical. It might be necessary to use decoupling capacitors at the input and output.

The best results are obtained when the input and carrier are simple. Complex waveshapes contain so many harmonics that the output can be quite noisy, but again experimentation will be your guide in your quest for new sounds.

When used with a voltage-controlled amplifier and exponential envelope, the ring modulator can produce excellent bell, gong, and chime sounds. When you use your voice, the result is an eerie conversation.

DIFFERENTIATOR

This circuit extracts a signal equal to the difference between input A and input B. In Fig. 9-8, inputs A and B are decoupled through capacitors C1 and C2. Potentiometers R1 and R2 provide amplitude control for both inputs while R3 and R4 prevent the circuit from being overdriven. Sounds produced by this circuit might resemble the ring modulator, but they are not as complex—in fact, the output is always less complex because it subtracts one input from the other. This module can be used to output a simpler, more musical signal from two complex or noisy signals.

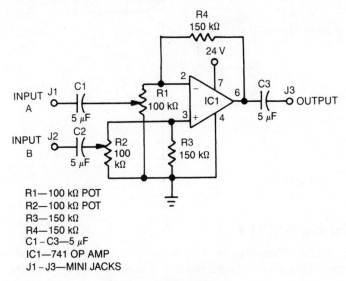

R1—100 kΩ POT
R2—100 kΩ POT
R3—150 kΩ
R4—150 kΩ
C1 – C3—5 µF
IC1—741 OP AMP
J1 – J3—MINI JACKS

Fig. 9-8. Differentiator.

INTEGRATOR

A square wave fed to an integrator converts to a triangular wave. The effect of the circuit is similar to a low-pass filter, but it is not as versatile because it is not voltage controlled. Figure 9-9 shows an integrated circuit amplifier with a capacitor, C4, in the feedback loop. This capacitor causes a lag in response and thus attenuates the high frequencies. Resistor R3 controls the circuit's gain, and capacitors C1, C2, and C3 serve as decouplers.

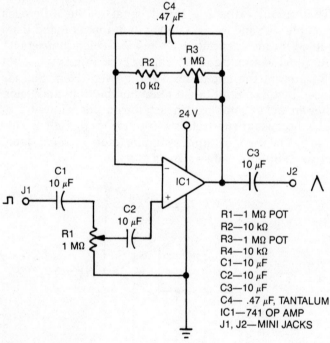

Fig. 9-9. Integrator.

PHASE SHIFTER

The schematic in Fig. 9-10 is a circuit designed to reverse the phase of an incoming waveshape. Transistor Q1 is an amplifier that occupies a center position with regard to

110

supply voltage and ground potential. The signal normally emanates from the positive side of the circuit, through capacitors C2 and C3. As a control voltage is applied to transistor Q2, the output shifts to the negative side of the circuit. The resultant sound is similar to that of pulse width modulation.

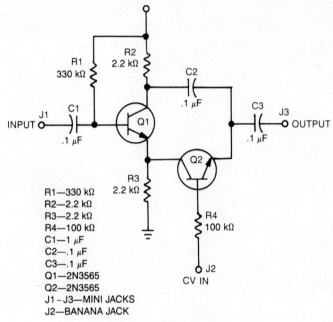

R1—330 kΩ
R2—2.2 kΩ
R3—2.2 kΩ
R4—100 kΩ
C1—1 μF
C2—.1 μF
C3—.1 μF
Q1—2N3565
Q2—2N3565
J1 – J3—MINI JACKS
J2—BANANA JACK

Fig. 9-10. Phase shifter.

System Planning

IF YOU PLAN TO BUILD A SYSTEM, THERE ARE a few things you should take into consideration. There are many elements involved in the construction of even a small system, so this chapter deals with tying all of those parts together.

CABINETS

You can build a large cabinet to allow for expansion (Fig. 10-1) or you might just want a few circuits in a small cabinet (Fig. 10-2). In either case (no pun intended), you need to select proper housing for your project.

Many synthesizer manufacturers build each module separately and then put them into a common cabinet. This system is not recommended for home-brew equipment because an enormous amount of work is involved in cutting each and every faceplate. The large system faceplate described in this chapter uses a 15-inch by 30-inch piece of 14-gauge sheet aluminum. The thickness of the metal is adequate for support yet thin enough to facilitate easy hole drilling. After you have chosen the module layout, draw the control locations with a pencil. Cabinet mounting screws should be placed about every 3 inches, and do not forget to secure the plate to

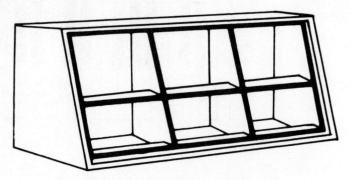

Fig. 10-1. Large system cabinet.

Fig. 10-2. Small system cabinet.

support posts or panels. It is very important to build a stable enclosure for your equipment, so if you feel you lack the carpentry skills, consider acquiring the services of a cabinet maker.

When drilling holes in the faceplate, it is a good idea to tap an indentation into the metal with a hammer and nail to prevent the drill bit from spinning out of position.

PANEL LABELING

The importance of control labeling, especially with large systems, is undeniable. Quick and accurate control manipulation is often required in electronic music composition, so clusters of unidentified controls can be both confusing and frustrating.

The easiest way to identify functions on a faceplate is to use press type, which can be found at any art supply store. To simplify this procedure, you can use abbreviations, shortened words, and symbols. Calibration lines, although useful, can also be omitted. After you have the graphics in place, spray or paint on a fixative to protect the surface.

KNOBS

Two sizes of knobs should be used: a small knob for presets and modules with lots of controls, and a larger knob for more accurate or frequent adjustments.

Knobs will be among your most expensive purchases, so it will be to your advantage to buy in large quantity if you decide to build a large system. Local supply houses might not stock the quantity you need, but you might get a discount if you specially order them.

CONTROLS

Toggle switches are expensive, but since slide switches require rectangular mounting holes, it is advised to use toggles. Miniature toggles take up less space and can also be purchased in quantity at local distributors.

There are two types of potentiometers: open and sealed. The open type are less expensive and can be cleaned if necessary with a quick shot of electronic spray cleaner.

INTERNAL CONNECTIONS

The faceplate should be connected to the ground or 0 volts terminal of the power supply. This allows the faceplate to act as a hum shield for the entire unit. Power connections to each circuit should be made with the use of barrier strips placed about every 8 inches or so. These strips provide power access to all circuits and prevent short circuits when connecting. Color-coded wire should be used to avoid mistakes (red for 15 volts, black for ground, yellow for 24 volts, green for 5 volts). Do not connect the wires directly to the barrier strips, but group them into bundles and run them along the sides of the cabinets, as in Fig. 10-3.

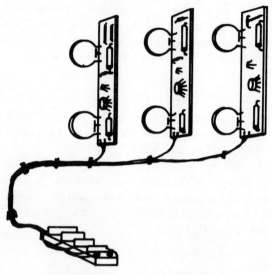

Fig. 10-3. Power wiring diagram.

LARGE SYSTEM LAYOUT

Because a synthesizer is a very complex device, a logical arrangement of modules is an absolute necessity. Figure 10-4 shows the front panel layout of the large system. A technique called *clustering* is used in large systems and involves the grouping of identical or similar modules in one section of the cabinet. All of the pitch-generating oscillators are located in the section lettered A. Letter B marks the area that contains the voltage-controlled amps with self-contained envelope generators. The sequencer, clock, and two glide modules are located in section C. A drive module is pictured in section D, while power is controlled in section E, which also includes the external keyboard access jacks. Section F groups four attenuators, and G contains a white noise generator and ring modulator. Section H contains a six-channel stereo mixer. Sections I and J display three voltage-controlled filters (bandpass, high pass, and low pass). A three-channel electronic switch and preamp occupy section K. Section L is a voltage-controlled reverb, and a small interface is in the area designated by letter M.

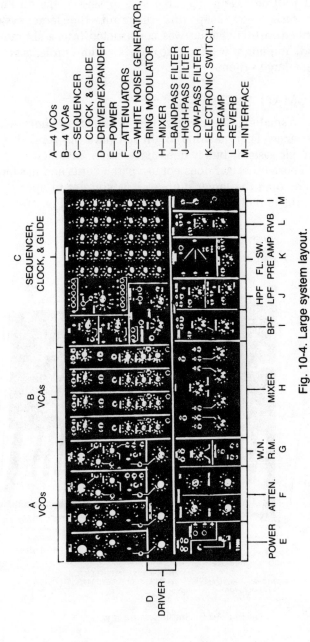

A—4 VCOs
B—4 VCAs
C—SEQUENCER
CLOCK, & GLIDE
D—DRIVER/EXPANDER
E—POWER
F—ATTENUATORS
G—WHITE NOISE GENERATOR,
RING MODULATOR
H—MIXER
I—BANDPASS FILTER
J—HIGH-PASS FILTER
LOW-PASS FILTER
K—ELECTRONIC SWITCH,
PREAMP
L—REVERB
M—INTERFACE

Fig. 10-4. Large system layout.

If putting together a large system seems like an enormous task, then keep this in mind—the large system described in this chapter was constructed over a six-month period. You might want to take on a few small projects before trying a large system.

THE SMALL SYSTEM

The smaller system in Fig. 10-5 is known as a *hard-wired synthesizer*. This machine might not have the versatility of the larger system, but it does have some advantages of its own. The synthesizer does not use patch cords and has fewer modules than the larger unit, so it is simpler to operate. A block diagram of the small system is shown in Fig. 10-6.

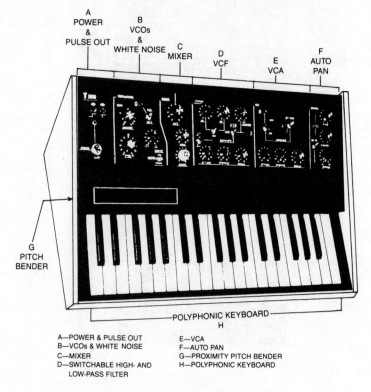

A—POWER & PULSE OUT
B—VCOs & WHITE NOISE
C—MIXER
D—SWITCHABLE HIGH- AND
LOW-PASS FILTER

E—VCA
F—AUTO PAN
G—PROXIMITY PITCH BENDER
H—POLYPHONIC KEYBOARD

Fig. 10-5. Small system layout.

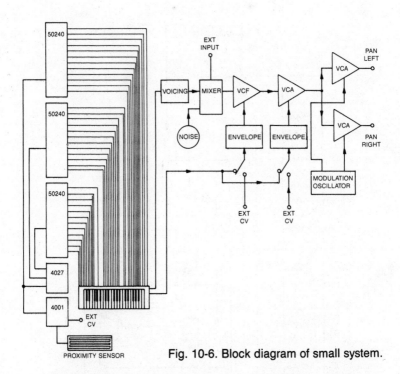

Fig. 10-6. Block diagram of small system.

Although this system has a lot in common with other hard-wired synthesizers, it has a few special features built into it. It can interface completely with the large system. The power switch and positive step and negative pulse outputs are included in section A. Section B shows an unusual method of generating tones called *top-octave* generation. A single square wave divides into a 12-tone diatonic scale, and as shown in Fig. 10-7, IC2 divides the original pitch further to produce two more octaves. There are several advantages to this approach, one being that you have a totally polyphonic keyboard (you can play as many keys at one time as you need).

PROXIMITY SENSOR

Because all pitches are derived from a single oscillator, a proximity sensor can be used to bend the pitch of the entire

119

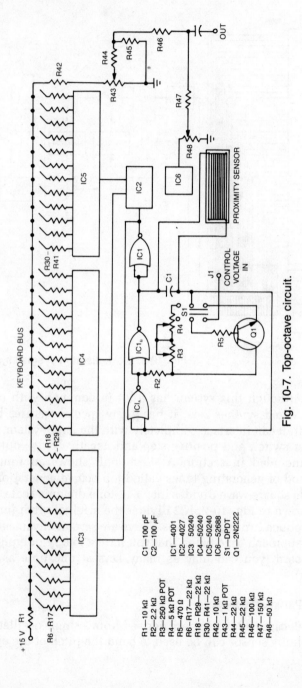

Fig. 10-7. Top-octave circuit.

R1—10 kΩ
R2—2.2 kΩ
R3—250 kΩ POT
R4—5 kΩ POT
R5—470 Ω
R6 – R17—22 kΩ
R18 – R29—22 kΩ
R30–R41—22 kΩ
R42—10 kΩ
R43—1 kΩ POT
R44—22 kΩ
R45—22 kΩ
R46—100 kΩ
R47—150 kΩ
R48—50 kΩ

C1—100 pF
C2—100 μF

IC1—4001
IC2—4027
IC3 50240
IC4—50240
IC5—50240
IC6—52688
S1—DPDT
Q1—2N2222

keyboard. The sensor is placed on the left side of the keyboard and is activated by placing your hand a few inches above the sensor. As you bring your hand closer to it, the pitch decends. When you touch the sensor, the effect is complete (pressure will not substantially increase the effect). The total range of the bend is approximately a major 4th. With just a few minutes of practice, you can master the playing technique of this sensor. Produce an ascending tone by placing your hand on the sensor before playing and then pulling it away. Vibrato and other modulating effects are easier to do on a device of this type, and you can develop plenty of new effects through experimentation.

Figure 10-8 shows an actual-size foil pattern of the proximity sensor. After etching this circuit, make sure you do not get a continuity reading between points A and B with an ohmmeter. Since the board is mounted outside the machine and your hand will come in contact with it, use a nail file or sandpaper to smooth the soldered points.

PROGRAMMABLE KEYBOARD

One other advantage of the small system is the programmable keyboard. This means that the keyboard will follow any control voltage that is input through S1 (of Fig. 10-7). Use a sequencer, for example, to control the pitch by connecting its output to the oscillator input. Press a key and tune the pitch with the sequencer until you have the desired number of stages. Now when a key is pressed, a sequence begins. Press a key that's a major 3rd higher, and the entire sequence changes to that pitch.

The programming diagram in Fig. 10-9 shows some other possibilities. Another control voltage operates the filter, and the pulse generator is triggering the envelope and voltage-controlled amplifier. A trigger output from the synthesizer is also controlling the pulse generator, or it can be used to control the sequencer directly. High-speed operation of this scheme can produce complex tambors using the same techniques described in Chapter 5 with even more spectacular results.

121

Fig. 10-8. Foil pattern of proximity sensor.

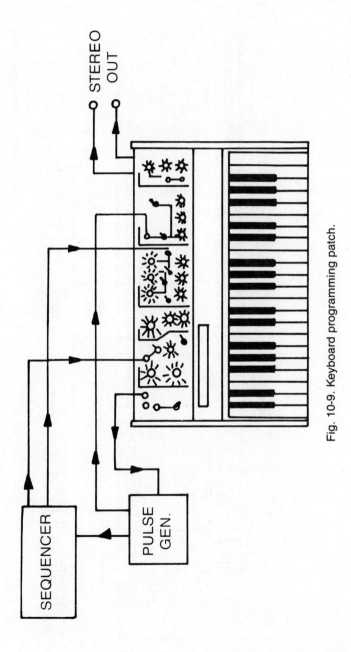

Fig. 10-9. Keyboard programming patch.

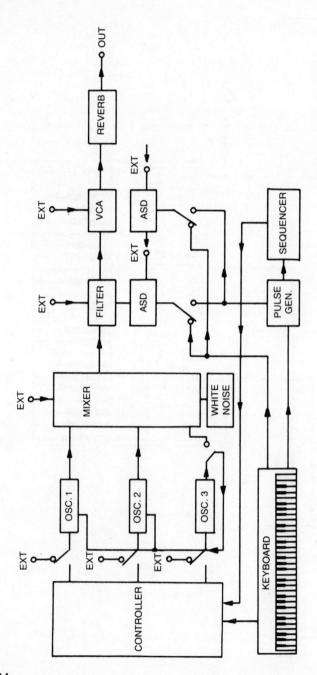

Fig. 10-10. Analog system layout.

LAYOUT

In addition to the pulse output and VCO section, there is a mixer with an external input in section C (of Fig. 10-5). Section D contains a voltage-controlled filter with envelope generator. A voltage-controlled amplifier is located in section E, and an auto panning module at letter F completes the panel layout. Section G is the proximity pitch bender, and letter H denotes the polyphonic keyboard.

A three-oscillator monophonic synthesizer is diagrammed in Fig. 10-10. It contains a pulse generator, a sequencer, and a reverberation unit, which are modules not usually associated with hard-wired synthesizers.

Musical Instrument Digital Interface (MIDI)

WHEN SYNTHESIZERS WERE FIRST MARKETed, manufacturers made no attempt to standardize electrical specifications. Because of this, synthesizers were considered too experimental and were relegated to the academic scene.

It was clear that if manufacturers were going to produce professionally viable equipment, they must develop a standardized interface. Hence, a system known as MIDI (musical instrument digital interface) was devised to provide a means of synchronizing activities.

A five-pin DIN plug was selected as the standard MIDI connector, but only pin 5 transmits data, which classifies this unit as using serial transmission. In addition to the conventional inputs and outputs, there is a MIDI THRU port that merely passes on any signal appearing at MIDI IN.

The MIDI system transmits a wealth of information. A pulse is sent whenever a key is pressed and also when released. If the synthesizer contains a rhythm generator, it produces a pulse train, and when activated, it cancels the pulses that emanate from the keyboard.

The MIDI system produces signals that communicate which key has been pressed, the velocity of attack, the

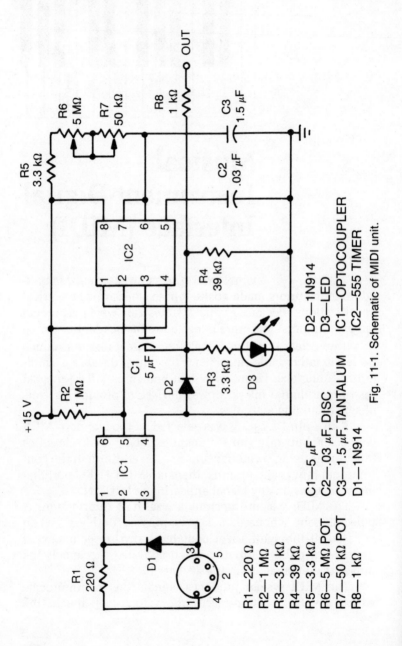

R1—220 Ω
R2—1 MΩ
R3—3.3 kΩ
R4—39 kΩ
R5—3.3 kΩ
R6—5 MΩ POT
R7—50 kΩ POT
R8—1 kΩ

C1—5 μF
C2—.03 μF, DISC
C3—1.5 μF, TANTALUM
D1—1N914

D2—1N914
D3—LED
IC1—OPTOCOUPLER
IC2—555 TIMER

Fig. 11-1. Schematic of MIDI unit.

128

amount of pressure placed on a key, and the position of any continuous controllers (pitch benders, modulation, etc.).

Figure 11-1 shows the schematic of a MIDI digital-to-analog interface, Fig. 11-2 shows a block diagram, and Fig. 11-3 shows the foil pattern. Most of the information processed by the MIDI system cannot be used by analog machines for any practical purpose. However, the keyboard pulses and pulse train information from rhythm generators can be extracted and used to provide an important communication link between digital and analog systems.

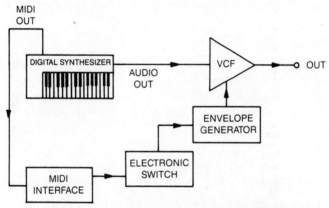

Fig. 11-2. Block diagram of analog control of digital tambor.

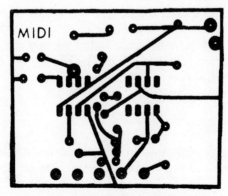

Fig. 11-3. Foil pattern of MIDI unit.

An optocoupler is used to prevent the transfer of noise and also to couple the 5-volt computer input to the power supply of the analog unit. IC2 is connected to the power by R2 and receives its required negative pulse from IC1. When used with a rhythm machine, R6 enables the selection of as many or as few sync pulses as needed. Resistor R7 is a fine-tuning control, and R5 prevents the power supply from shorting. The output of IC2 is decoupled through C1 and is monitored by D3. Diode D2 clamps negative voltage spikes to ground and R4 plus R8 establish ground reference and current limiting respectively. Capacitor C2 stabilizes the internal voltage divider in IC2 and eliminates false triggering.

OPERATION

A rhythm generator produces a fast, steady pulse train at its MIDI output. The optocoupler responds to all of these, so it is the function of the 555 timer to selectively ignore all but the pulses needed. It might take a little practice to master this tuning technique, but you might find that because of its versatility, you want to use it all the time.

THE KEYBOARD

Using a keyboard is somewhat different, because a pulse is produced when you press a key and another is generated when you release the key. There are two ways you can avoid the second pulse, and the first is to tune the interface. This method is best suited to regular rhythmic play due to the fixed setting of the MIDI unit. Using an electronic switch is another way, but remember to release the key before pressing the next. Finally, you can ignore compensation altogether for random or spontaneous effects.

APPLICATIONS

The block diagrams in the remainder of this chapter illustrate just a few of the possibilities, and experimentation

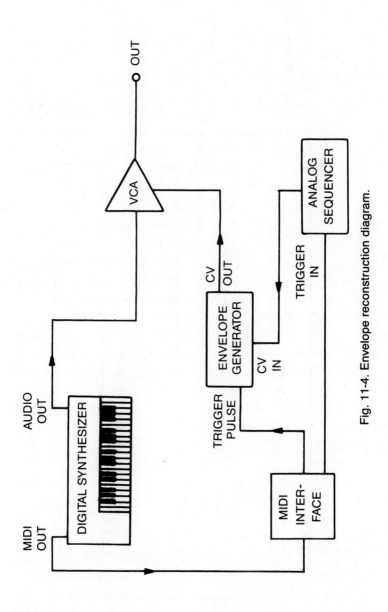

Fig. 11-4. Envelope reconstruction diagram.

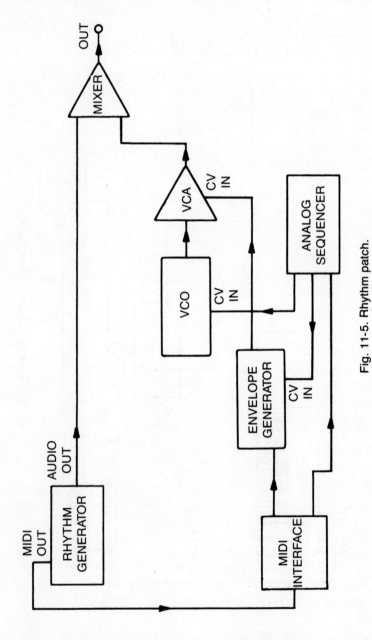

Fig. 11-5. Rhythm patch.

will reveal many more. One very important use for this circuit is *envelope reconstruction*, shown in Fig. 11-4. By combining both techniques, you have the incredible tone-generating capacity of digital and the envelope-generating and tone-modulating capabilities of analog.

LIGHTING SYSTEMS

Many performers use elaborate light shows to enhance their stage performance. The MIDI unit can afford the lighting director an expanded measure of control and synchronization. The coordination of strobe lights with rhythm, the triggering of movement in motorized light assemblies, and initiation of intensity changes in computer-controlled light systems are just a few of the possibilities for this MIDI system. See Figs. 11-5 and 11-6.

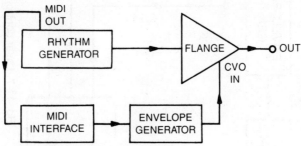

Fig. 11-6. Synchronized rhythm flange.

LASER SYSTEMS

Laser equipment is especially adaptable to use with the MIDI because it is completely compatible with the scanner systems used in laser light shows. See Fig. 11-7. Direct electronic music interfacing as well as digital synthesizer-to-computer control interfacing is possible. When the MIDI is combined with an envelope generator, image size can be controlled by music intensity, which can make a more convincing audio-visual display. There seems to be an almost limitless number of ways that the MIDI system can be applied to laser scanning systems.

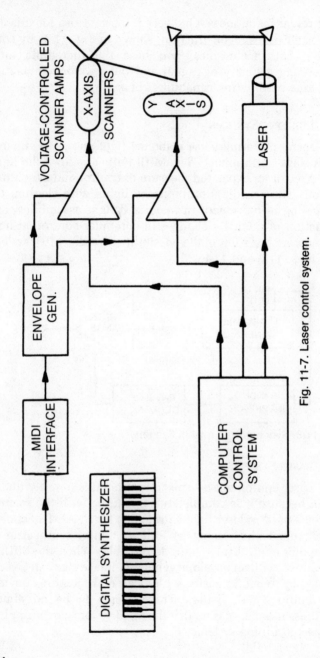

Fig. 11-7. Laser control system.

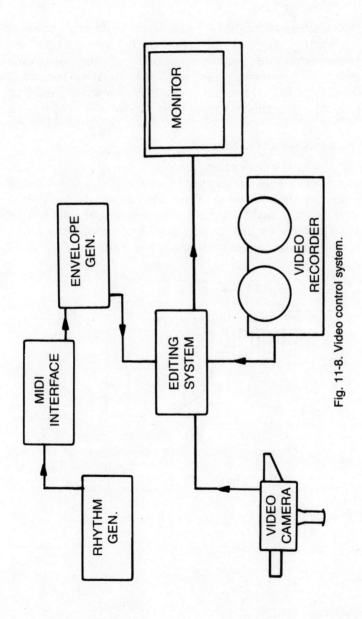

Fig. 11-8. Video control system.

VIDEO SYSTEMS

Although it might be necessary to build other interfacing circuits, such as voltage-controlled video amplifiers, voltage-controlled envelope generators, and electronic switches, it is nonetheless possible to enlist an incredible control facility. Music video production studios would be particularly interested in this type interface. See Fig. 11-8.

MOTION PICTURE SYSTEMS

Motion picture studios are now using dialogue replacement systems and sampling keyboards that are already geared to MIDI operation. Samplers sometimes need envelope or tonal modification to ensure a natural sound. This MIDI system can provide any degree of change you might need to obtain desired results. See Fig. 11-9.

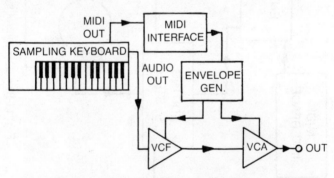

Fig. 11-9. Motion picture dialogue replacement diagram.

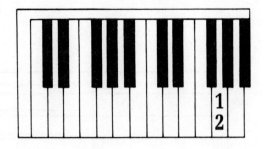

Digital
Synthesizers

ALL DIGITAL SYNTHESIZERS PROCESS THEIR
sounds with small built-in computers designed to use some
form of modulation to call up information. Computers are
high-speed counting devices that perceive the world by continually measuring the state of the input. This measuring
process is known as *sampling*, and there are a number of different methods.

MODULATION

There are four types of pulse modulation, each of which
is described in this section. They are pulse width, position,
amplitude, and code modulation.

PULSE WIDTH MODULATION

The voltage-controlled oscillator in Chapter 2 controls
the width of its pulse output by varying the amplitude of the
analog input. Digital processing makes amplitude changes
in analog waveshapes with changes in the pulse width of the
sampling frequency. Figure 12-1 shows a graphic representation of this process, showing the causal relationship between
waveshapes.

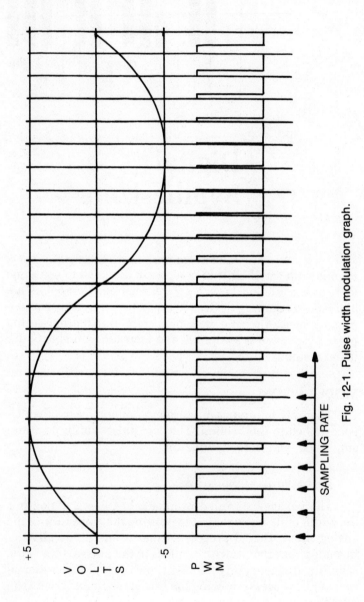

Fig. 12-1. Pulse width modulation graph.

PULSE POSITION MODULATION

Another type of modulation changes the position of a fixed-width pulse. This system is called pulse position modulation and is illustrated in Fig. 12-2. As the graph shows, the pulse width remains constant but changes position within the sampling frame.

PULSE AMPLITUDE MODULATION

A third type of modulation does not involve the position or the width of the pulse but instead involves the amplitude of the pulse. Figure 12-3 shows that this type of modulation is a clear case of cause and effect. This type of modulation is also used with the ring modulator in Chapter 9. Very-low-frequency amplitude modulation is accomplished with the envelope generator.

PULSE CODE MODULATION

One of the most popular systems of synthesizer processing is pulse code modulation. This technique involves a four-bit binary system. When viewed graphically (Fig. 12-4), it seems to lack the causal coordination that is present in the other systems. A second look, however, shows that when the sine wave is at its peak, bits 0, 1, and 2 are all low. When the sine wave is at its lowest point, bits 0, 1, and 2 are all high. Therefore, there is a causal mechanism—it's just harder to perceive because of the multiple-element programming.

OTHER TECHNIQUES

Several other digital techniques are described herein including linear arithmetic, cross wave, MIDI, and sampling.

LINEAR ARITHMETIC

Linear arithmetic methods produce sound by selecting and mixing *partials*, which are PCM samples or digitally

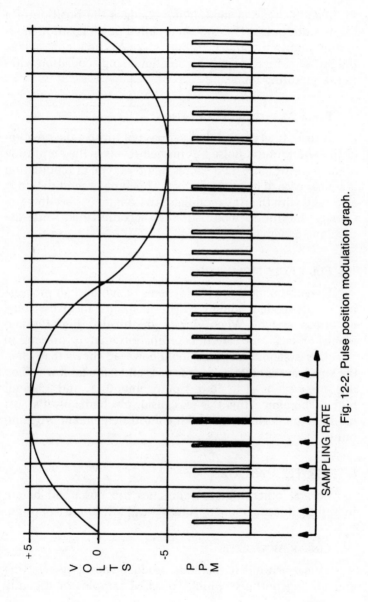

Fig. 12-2. Pulse position modulation graph.

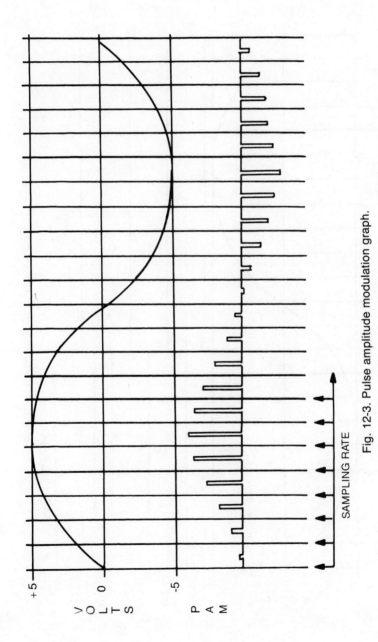

Fig. 12-3. Pulse amplitude modulation graph.

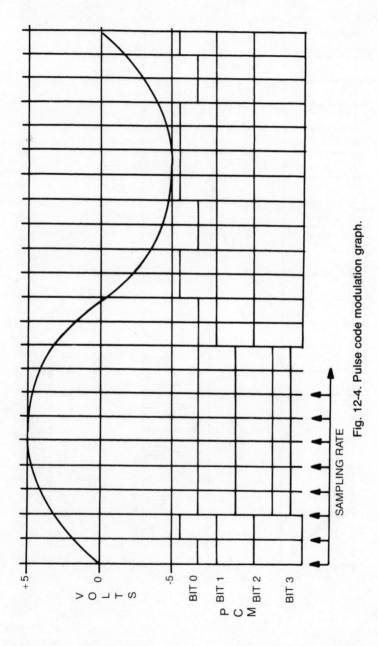

Fig. 12-4. Pulse code modulation graph.

synthesized waveshapes. Partials are single-element parameters such as attack, sustain, tonalities, and harmonics. When these elements are combined, they form a complete sound that is ready for further processing.

CROSS WAVE

Cross wave synthesis is an envelope-generating process that crossfades attack and sustain waves to create complex envelope signals.

MIDI

The previous chapter discussed the MIDI system in some detail. Digital synthesizers produce signals that communicate to other digital synthesizers. The MIDI system is the only system that digital machines recognize, but this is not such a handicap because the sound output of the digital synthesizer can be processed by analog or digital equipment.

SAMPLING

One of the most useful devices to come out of digital research is the *sampling keyboard*. Many types and sizes are commercially available, and they have become a standard item in sound studios.

There are two basic types of sampling: *momentary* and *continuous*. Momentary sounds, such as a single drum beat, contain their own natural envelope that includes pitch information. A sample played back reproduces with amazing accuracy, however, if you press another key to change the pitch, the envelope also changes. In nature, frequencies change quite readily, but for the most part, envelopes do not. Therefore, the envelope reconstruction patch (Chapter 11, Fig. 11-2) was devised. Samplers do have some envelope modifying ability, but the sampler's computer will still make envelope changes to accommodate increased envelope time.

When sampling a continuous tone, sound the tone before pressing the sampling button and keep the tone on for the entire sampling period. A process called *looping* allows you to hold the tone for as long as the key is pressed. An audible "bump" sometimes occurs due to phase, pitch, or amplitude changes that took place during sampling. The best way to avoid this is to provide a consistent sampling source or take a longer sample. Some of the more sophisticated machines have the ability to eliminate "looping bumps" as well as other inherent sampling problems.

One possible problem is when the sampling frequency is an exact multiple (harmonic) of the frequency to be sampled. Even if the match is not exact, there is a potential for creating beat frequencies and sideband modulation. Computers can usually avoid this kind of distortion because their output is just a stored digital representation of the input and cannot interact. However, when an input is exactly in phase with the sampling frequency (commonly known as a glitch), the computer can misinterpret the input.

The filters in Chapter 3 can be MIDI interlocked and high-speed operated to eliminate sampling distortions and still maintain tonal integrity. Some very expensive sampling keyboards measure their sampling time in minutes rather than seconds, which eliminates certain continuity problems, but the emphasis here is to find practical solutions to the inherent problems of more affordable or accessible samplers.

Any sound can be sampled, but by far the most important source for sampling is analog synthesizers. The combination of oscillators, filters, flangers, sequencers, and MIDI equipment provide an endless supply of complex, harmonically rich, and uncompromised material.

When it comes to the quick and easy production of complex tonalities, it is the analog system that is superior, but high-speed processing and information storage is better suited to digital. It is the combination of analog and digital technologies that maximize the control and enhance the capabilities of the composer/musician.

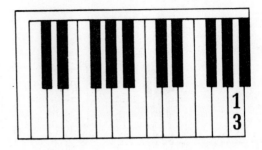

Parts
Identification

SINCE MANUFACTURERS HAVE NOT STANDAR-
dized parts to a large degree, it has become necessary for the
technician to familiarize himself or herself with a very wide
variety of component types. This chapter is simply a listing
of most of the different components and can help with such
questions as lead identification and component layout to prevent mistakes and eliminate frustration.

VOLTAGE REGULATORS

There are three basic types of regulator cases as shown in
Fig. 13-1. The most popular voltages are 5, 12, and 15 volts
at about 1 ampere of current. It is a good idea to connect a
heatsink to the regulator to assure its cool operation.

TRANSISTORS

Bipolar and field-effect transistors come in a wide variety of cases and pin arrangements (Figs. 13-2 and 13-3). The
base lead of a bipolar transistor is almost always in the center,
but there are exceptions to the rule, so when testing
unmarked transistors, try all combinations before making a
determination. If the lead arrangement of a transistor does

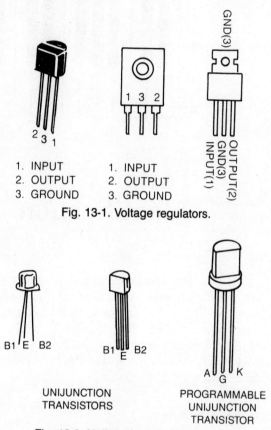

Fig. 13-1. Voltage regulators.

1. INPUT
2. OUTPUT
3. GROUND

1. INPUT
2. OUTPUT
3. GROUND

GND(3)

OUTPUT(2)
GND(3)
INPUT(1)

B1 E B2

B1 E B2

A G K

UNIJUNCTION
TRANSISTORS

PROGRAMMABLE
UNIJUNCTION
TRANSISTOR

Fig. 13-2. Unijunction transistor cases.

not match the configuration required on the circuit board, try making lead modifications like those in Fig. 13-4.

Field-effect transistors often have their gate lead on one side, and since FETs are electrically symmetrical (their source and drain leads are interchangeable), there should be no problem with lead placement.

INTEGRATED CIRCUITS

Sockets should be used with integrated circuits to avoid heat damage or other complications. As shown in Fig. 13-5,

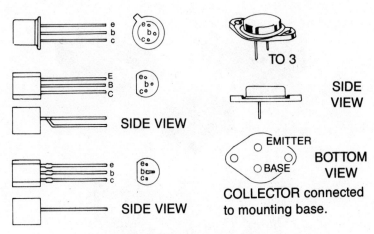

Fig. 13-3. Transistor case types.

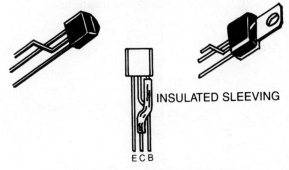

Fig. 13-4. Transistor lead modification.

sockets are available for any pin arrangement or size and they are inexpensive.

A variety of integrated circuits are incorporated in the designs in this book, so this section covers important considerations and information about these components.

VOLTAGE-CONTROLLED OSCILLATOR

The 566 is very useful as a low-frequency oscillator because of its triangular output, which is necessary for flanging, panning, and vibrato (Fig. 13-6). It should not be used

Fig. 13-5. Sockets for integrated circuits.

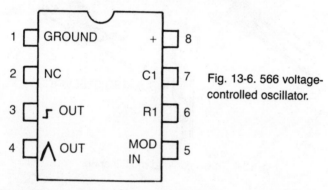

Fig. 13-6. 566 voltage-controlled oscillator.

as a prime audio source, however, because it lacks the saw-tooth waveshape, and the amplitude of the triangular wave is too low.

OPERATIONAL AMPLIFIER

The 741 operational amplifier is without a doubt the most popular linear integrated circuit in all of electronics. It is a high-gain device that lends itself to multiplicity of situations. It can function as an integrator, a differentiator, a filter, a flanger, or almost anything that comes to mind.

148

An exact gain ratio can be achieved with the selection of proper input and feedback resistors. Although the 741 was designed to operate with a dual power supply, it can easily be adapted to a single ended supply. Operational amplifiers are shown in Fig. 13-7.

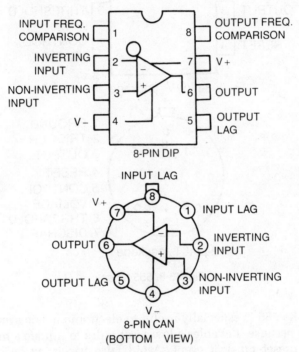

Fig. 13-7. Operational amplifiers.

TIMERS

The 555 timer is the perfect device for isolating timing events (Fig. 13-8). A negative pulse is required to trigger the timer, and the output pulse width is independent of the input. The output level equals the power supply voltage, so a current-limiting resistor, at the output, is necessary. Pin 7 is at ground potential during part of the cycle, so it should never be allowed direct access to full power.

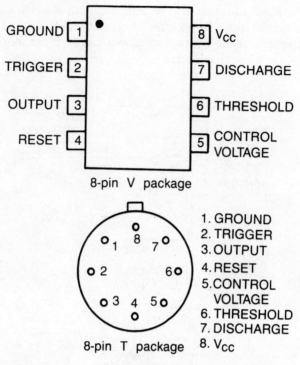

GROUND 1   8 V$_{CC}$

TRIGGER 2   7 DISCHARGE

OUTPUT 3   6 THRESHOLD

RESET 4   5 CONTROL VOLTAGE

8-pin V package

1. GROUND
2. TRIGGER
3. OUTPUT
4. RESET
5. CONTROL VOLTAGE
6. THRESHOLD
7. DISCHARGE
8. V$_{CC}$

8-pin T package

Fig. 13-8. 555 timer.

The 555 is especially useful to electronic music synthesizers because it enables a low-level pulse to initiate a high-level preset musical event. Avoid false triggering by connecting a small capacitor across pin 5 to ground. A dual timer is also available—the 556. Both single and dual timers can be used with power supplies ranging from 3 to 15 volts. If pin 6 is connected to pin 2, the timer will function as an oscillator with a pulse output equal to the full range of the power supply.

QUAD NOR GATE

This integrated circuit contains four independent gates, which when cascaded (as in Chapter 2, Fig. 2-13) can function as a pulse generator. It is often used as the drive element for dual analog delay lines. See Fig. 13-9.

Other applications for this unit are a switch debouncer, pulse isolator, pulse inverter, pulse clock, and as a drive unit for top-octave generators. The gates can be paralleled to increase current-handling capacity. Although this device was designed to operate as a digital processor, it can function as a linear amplifier. Remember to observe all handling precautions for CMOS integrated circuits and other digital devices.

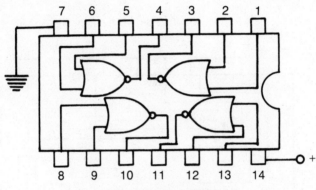

Fig. 13-9. 4001 quad NOR gate.

DUAL D FLIP-FLOP

The 4013 is used mostly as a frequency divider in electronic music synthesizers, and it was chosen to supply the alternate pulse outputs for the pulse clock in Chapter 2. See Fig. 13-10.

DUAL J-K FLIP-FLOP

The 4027 is similar to the 4013, but there are two important differences: the J-K flip-flop has 16 pins, and all of the inputs must be used. A 4027 is used to derive the two lower octaves of the top-octave circuit in Chapter 10. See Fig. 13-11.

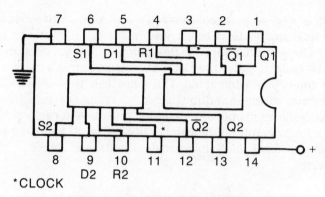

Fig. 13-10. 4013 dual D flip-flop.

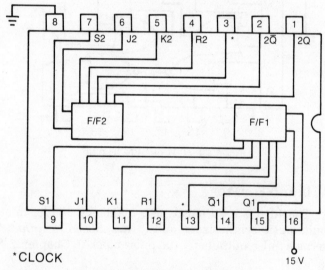

Fig. 13-11. 4027 dual J-K flip-flop.

DECADE COUNTER

The 4017 is one of the most versatile of all CMOS integrated circuits (Fig. 13-12). It can produce control voltages directly from its outputs, thereby eliminating the need for elaborate isolation circuits. You can select the number of stages and at any time reset the counter with an external signal. The IC can be triggered by a wide range of pulse amplitudes. The counter operates on as little as 3 or as much as 15 volts, and it consumes very little power. The 4017 exhibits a stability that can assure the builder of a successful project.

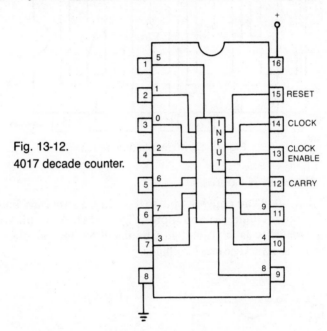

Fig. 13-12.
4017 decade counter.

QUAD BILATERAL SWITCH

The 4066 contains four independent switches capable of passing analog or digital signals (Fig. 13-13). A switch is activated by applying a voltage (equal to or nearly equal to the supply voltage) to a control input. When a switch is on, its resistance to the passage of signal is approximately 300 ohms, and when it is off, the resistance is 10^{12} ohms. These specifications make the 4066 ideally suited to the job of signal routing.

In Chapter 6, the 4066 is used in an electronic switch circuit that can pass audio signals, control voltages, and even MIDI signals, and since the circuit is bilateral, inputs and outputs are interchangable.

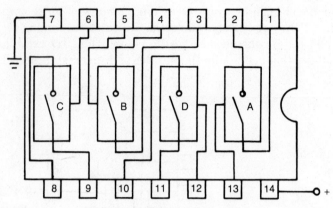

Fig. 13-13. 4066 bilateral switch.

DIVIDE BY N COUNTER

The 4018 can convert a pulse train into a sine wave equal to $1/10$ the frequency of the input (Fig. 13-14). A circuit with this capability is included in Chapter 6 for the purpose of producing sweep control voltages.

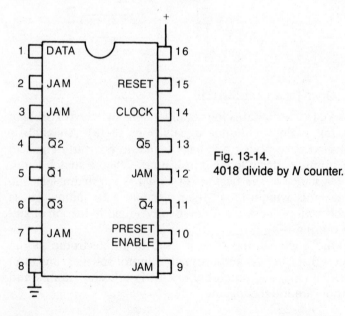

Fig. 13-14.
4018 divide by N counter.

BINARY COUNTER

The 4024 can produce outputs of 1, 2, and 3 octaves lower than the input frequency (Fig. 13-15). The only requirement imposed is that the input must be a square wave. In Chapter 9, the circuit labeled "octavizer" performs these pitch reduction services quite competently.

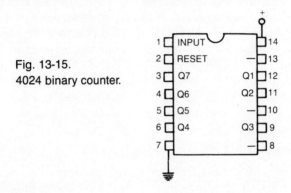

Fig. 13-15.
4024 binary counter.

DIODES

Diodes determine the directional flow of current and can prevent the interaction of components or circuits tied to a common point. They come in a variety of case types, as Fig. 13-16 illustrates. Zener diodes, unlike conventional diodes, conduct in reverse when a specific breakdown voltage is reached, which makes them well suited to voltage regulator circuits. Tunnel diodes contain impurities in their p-type

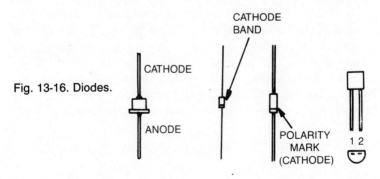

Fig. 13-16. Diodes.

155

and n-type materials, so electrical charges pass across the junction by an action called "tunneling," which creates a negative-resistance region that permits amplification.

OPTICAL DEVICES

Figure 13-17 displays several optical units that are used in circuits throughout this book. The optocoupler is actually a light-emitting diode (LED) and a phototransistor in a light-tight package. This arrangement allows one power loop to control another power loop without any actual electrical connection.

Light-emitting diodes serve as indicators and can duplicate the action of the optocoupler if enclosed in a light-tight package with a phototransistor or photocell.

RESISTORS

The most common element in almost every circuit is the resistor. It tailors voltage and manipulates current to facilitate any design situation. Resistors come in a wide range of values that are identified by colored bands. The color code is shown in Fig. 13-18. If resistors are in series, the total resistance is equal to the sum of all the resistor values. To calculate the total resistance of two resistors in parallel, use this formula:

$$\frac{R1 \times R2}{R1 + R2}$$

If you need an odd-value resistor, select a lower-value carbon resistor and file it (as shown in Fig. 13-19) until it increases to the necessary value. Use a digital multimeter to keep track of the changing resistance while filling. When you reach the desired value, apply a coat of modeling cement or paint to the resistor to prevent moisture from affecting its value. All resistors are $1/4$ watt unless otherwise stated.

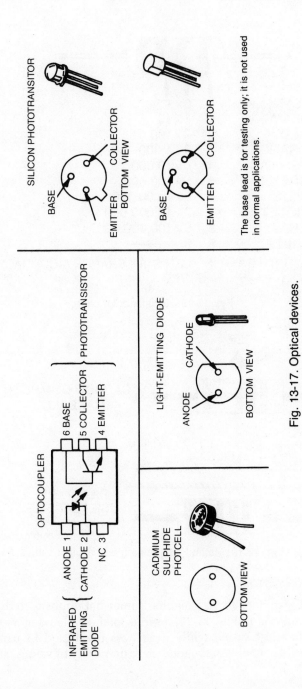

Fig. 13-17. Optical devices.

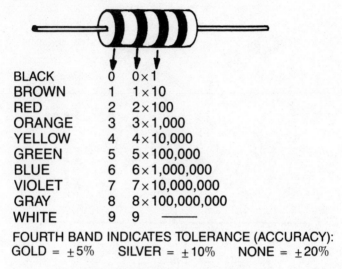

BLACK	0	0×1
BROWN	1	1×10
RED	2	2×100
ORANGE	3	3×1,000
YELLOW	4	4×10,000
GREEN	5	5×100,000
BLUE	6	6×1,000,000
VIOLET	7	7×10,000,000
GRAY	8	8×100,000,000
WHITE	9	9 ——

FOURTH BAND INDICATES TOLERANCE (ACCURACY):
GOLD = ±5%   SILVER = ±10%   NONE = ±20%

Fig. 13-18. Resistor color code.

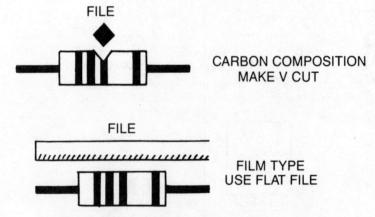

FILE

CARBON COMPOSITION
MAKE V CUT

FILE

FILM TYPE
USE FLAT FILE

Fig. 13-19. Method for attaining odd resistor values.

CAPACITORS

Capacitors act in a manner somewhat opposite to that of resistors. As in Fig. 13-20, a series total equals no more than the smallest value, while capacitors connected in parallel add values to obtain the total. A wide variety of values, sizes,

158

and case types (Fig. 13-21), are available at all electronic suppliers. If polarity is a factor in the use of a capacitor, it will be indicated on the device and should be used accordingly. Voltage ratings of electrolytic capacitors should exceed the power supply voltage. Situations that require precise values with low leakage should employ tantalum capacitors.

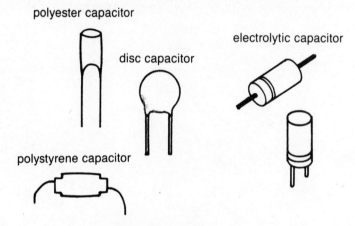

Fig. 13-20. Capacitor types.

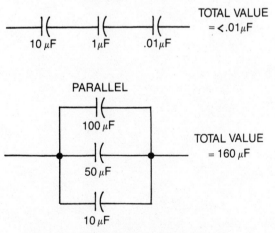

Fig. 13-21. Capacitor operating principals.

159

Index

A

adjustable ring modulator, 89
ambience recovery system, 42, 44, 45
amplifiers, 35-45
  ambience recovery system, 42, 44-45
  mixers, 40
  operational (*see* op amps)
  preamps, 35-36
  speakers and, 35, 40
  transconductance, 39
  voltage-controlled, 36-40, 47
amplitude modulation, 16
arithmetic, linear, digital synthesizers and, 139, 143
ASD units, 47
attack time, 47, 143
attenuators, 83-91
  adjustable ring modulator, 89
  crossfade diagram, 88, 89
  decoupling, 90, 95
  dual, 84
  feedback attenuation, 91
  frequency-crossing diagram, 85
  manual filter sweep, 86
  manual pan diagram, 86
  open, 88, 89
  sequencers and, 91
  speed-and pitch-coordinating diagram, 85
  synchronous, 87, 88
auto pan, 105, 106

B

band reject filters, 32
bandpass filters, 26
bilateral switch, quad, 153, 154
binary counter, 155
bipolar transistors, 145
  negative resistance in, 13
  substitutions for, 5
  tester for, 8-10

C

cabinets, 113
cables, 4
capacitors, 158
  altering tonal quality of sources with, 25
  filter capability of, 26
  operating principals of, 159
  substitutions for, 5
  types of, 159
circuit boards, 5
circuit designer, 5-7
clock pulse, 20-22